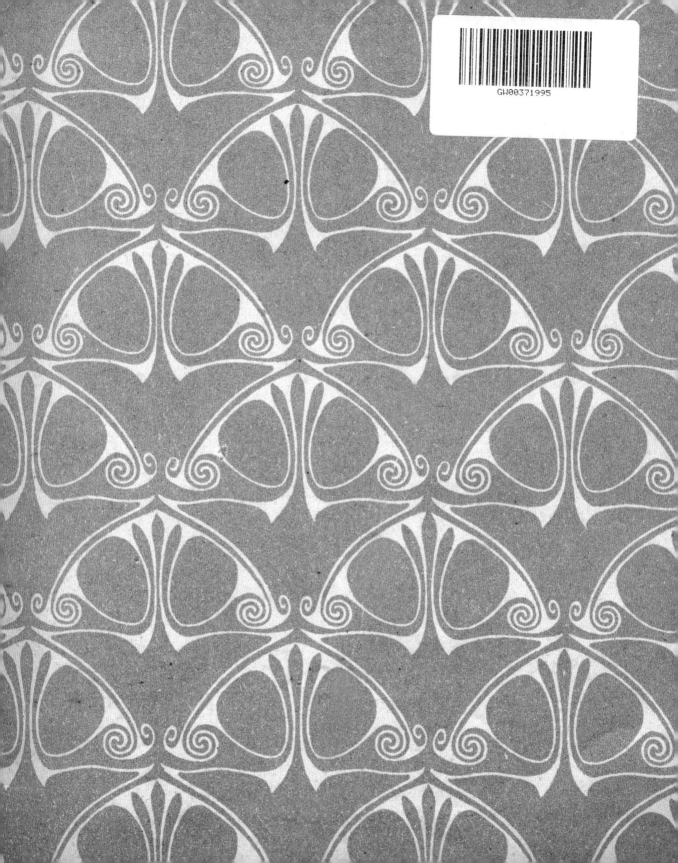

The Basic Cookbook

The Basic Cookbook

compiled by **LESLEY PAGETT**

NEW HOLLAND

Published in 2013 by
New Holland Publishers
London • Sydney • Auckland

First published in 2004
The Chandlery Unit 114 50 Westminster Bridge Road London SE1 7QY
1/66 Gibbes Street Chatswood NSW 2067 Australia
218 Lake Road Northcote Auckland New Zealand

www.newhollandpublishers.com

A catalogue record of this book is available at the British Library
and the National Library of Australia.

ISBN: 9781742574660

Publisher: Fiona Schultz
Design: Lorena Susak
Production Director: Olga Dementiev
Printer: Toppan Leefung Printing Ltd (China)

10 9 8 7 6 5 4 3 2

Follow New Holland Publishers on
Facebook: www.facebook.com/NewHollandPublishers

Contents

ACKNOWLEDGEMENTS

After many years of cooking for my children, I was thrilled to be given the opportunity to publish some of the recipes I had prepared for them with so much love. Thank you Nathan, Catherine and Adam – you have been rays of sunshine in my life. When having families of your own, I hope these recipes will be passed down to your children, too. To my mum and dad, Vera and Les, my sister Susan, my brother David, and all the fantastic friends with whom we enjoyed Gourmet Club and special dinners for so long, thank you for all your support and encouragement, and for believing in my ability to conquer.

Lesley

INTRODUCTION

In today's busy world, many of us have forgotten what basic, nutritious home cooking used to be—the food that our mothers and grandmothers prepared in the kitchen from scratch, and the recipes they passed down from generation to generation—dishes that were comforting, delicious and full of goodness.

The Basic Cookbook is a collection of those versatile and simple recipes you grew up with, and how to successfully cook them at home. Being practical and accessible, this cookbook also details directions for the novice cook on how to cook rice, scramble eggs, make stock and bake a cake—and features those all-important conversion charts to ensure that you get the recipe right the first time around. It also contains classic recipes that have stood the test of time—pumpkin soup, shepherd's pie, coleslaw and cheesecake, as well as the delicious curries, stir-fries and casseroles that people enjoy eating today.

So whether you are leaving home and want to learn how to cook, or you just want to create those nostalgic dishes from your childhood, we hope that *The Basic Cookbook* will enable you to enjoy good food at homewith great results.

Soups

* CAULIFLOWER SOUP *

1 cauliflower, broken into
  florets
3 large potatoes, peeled and
  cut into chunks
750 ml (3 cups) chicken stock
  (see page 380), or water
1 large onion, chopped
2 carrots, chopped
salt and freshly ground black
  pepper, to taste
1 x 300 g (1¼ cups) sour
  cream

serves 4–6

Cover cauliflower and potato in chicken stock or water in a pot and boil until soft. Mash vegetables with the liquid, making sure you use enough water to have the consistency of thick soup.

Add onion and carrot to soup. Simmer for 10 minutes. Puree the mixture in a blender or use a bar mix until smooth.

Just before serving, season with salt and pepper and stir in the sour cream. Serve hot with crusty French bread.

* CHICKEN NOODLE SOUP *

900 ml (3⅔ cups) chicken
  stock (see page 380)
1 bay leaf
1 onion, halved
250 g (8 oz) skinless chicken
  breast
60 g (2 oz) vermicelli,
  broken into smaller pieces
  (see glossary)
salt and freshly ground black
  pepper, to taste
1 tablespoon fresh parsley,
  chopped, to garnish

serves 4–6

Put chicken stock, bay leaf, onion and chicken breast into a large saucepan over a high heat. Cook until the mixture is boiling, stirring once or twice. Reduce heat to a simmer and cook for 10 minutes or until chicken is tender.

Lift chicken out of the saucepan with a draining spoon and cut into very small pieces. Lift out onion and bay leaf and discard. Bring stock back to the boil, add vermicelli and cook for 7 minutes or until al dente. Return chopped chicken to the pan and season with salt and pepper, then heat through.

Ladle into warm soup bowls and sprinkle with chopped parsley to serve.

* CHICKEN AND PINK PEPPERCORN SOUP *

60 g (2 oz) butter
½ capsicum (bell pepper),
    seeds and pith removed and
    finely chopped
45 g (1½ oz) plain (all-
    purpose) flour
750 ml (3 cups) chicken
    stock (see page 380)
375 ml (1½ cups) milk
125 ml (½ cup) white wine
1 tablespoon Dijon mustard
125 g (4 oz) button
    mushrooms, sliced
1½ tablespoons tomato paste
1 tablespoon pink
    peppercorns (see glossary)
1 tablespoon chives, chopped
1½ cups cooked chicken,
    finely chopped
125 ml (½ cup) fresh cream
freshly ground black pepper,
    to taste
salt (optional)

serves 6–8

Put chicken stock, bay leaf, onion and chicken breast into a large saucepan over a high heat. Cook until the mixture is boiling, stirring once or twice. Reduce heat to a simmer and cook for 10 minutes or until chicken is tender.

Lift chicken out of the saucepan with a draining spoon and cut into very small pieces. Lift out onion and bay leaf and discard. Bring stock back to the boil, add vermicelli and cook for 7 minutes or until al dente. Return chopped chicken to the pan and season with salt and pepper, then heat through.

Ladle into warm soup bowls and sprinkle with chopped parsley to serve.

* CORN AND CRAB BISQUE *

30 g (1 oz) butter
1 teaspoon curry powder
1 x 485 g (15½ oz) can
  cream of chicken soup
500 ml (2 cups) milk
1 x 250 g (8 oz) can creamy
  sweet corn
1 x 205 g (6½ oz) can
  crabmeat, shredded
salt and black pepper, to taste
1 chilli, sliced (optional)
crusty French bread, for
  serving

serves 6

In a large saucepan, melt butter, add curry powder and fry over a low heat for 1–2 minutes. Add chicken soup and milk, stirring continuously until well blended.

Add sweet corn and bring to the boil. Add shredded crabmeat and season with salt and pepper. Stir in the sliced chilli, if using.

Serve hot with crusty bread.

* CREAM OF CHICKEN SOUP *

60 g (2 oz) butter
4 tablespoons plain (all-
  purpose) flour
1.25 L (2 pints) chicken
  stock (see page 380)
625 ml (1 pint) scalded milk
  (or ½ milk and ½ cream)
1 chicken breast, shredded
1 small stalk celery, finely
  chopped
few drops tabasco sauce
salt and freshly ground black
  pepper, to taste
2 egg yolks
fresh chives, chopped, to serve

serves 4

Melt butter in a large saucepan, stir in flour and cook for about 1 minute, then add 625 ml (1 pint) of chicken stock. Stir continuously over medium heat until boiling. Add remaining stock, milk, chicken, celery, tabasco sauce and salt and pepper and bring to the boil. Reduce heat and simmer, covered, for 5 minutes.

In a bowl, beat egg yolks well with a fork, then pour into a heated tureen. Pour soup very slowly over egg yolks, stirring all the time with a wooden spoon.

Sprinkle with some fresh chives. Serve immediately.

* CREAM OF MUSHROOM SOUP *

250 g (8 oz) mushrooms
125 g (4 oz) butter
½ teaspoon salt
freshly ground black pepper,
   to taste
3 cloves garlic, finely chopped
1.25 L (5 cups) chicken stock
   (see page 380)
150 ml (½ cup) fresh cream,
   at room temperature
garlic-flavoured croutons, for
   serving (see page 27)
parsley, chopped

serves 4

Before cooking mushrooms, select some of the smallest ones and take a slice from the centre of each so that you have the outline of the mushroom. Put aside to garnish.

Wash mushrooms (do not peel them) and thinly slice. In a frying pan, heat butter to sizzling, then fry mushrooms with salt and a good grind of fresh pepper. Cool, then purée in a blender or food processor with garlic and 250 ml (1 cup) stock.

Pour remaining stock into a large saucepan. Add purée and heat soup to simmering point. Stir in cream. Add reserved mushroom slices and simmer soup for 5 minutes. Taste and adjust seasoning if necessary.

Serve hot with garlic-flavoured croutons and a sprinkle of parsley.

* CREAMY CHICKEN AND VEGETABLE SOUP *

1 roast chicken carcass
900 ml (3⅔ cups) water
1 bay leaf
1 chicken stock cube
salt and freshly ground black
  pepper, to taste
4 tablespoons fresh cream
2 tablespoons plain (all-
  purpose) flour
125 g (4 oz) mixed
  vegetables, cooked and
  chopped (if you have
  leftover vegetables from
  a roast, these would be
  perfect)

serves 4–6

Break chicken carcass into pieces and place in a large saucepan. Cover with water, add bay leaf, stock cube and salt and pepper. Bring to the boil over a high heat, then turn down heat to a simmer. Add cream and flour, stir through, cover with a lid and cook for 1 hour.

Drain contents of saucepan through a colander into a large bowl, then return liquid to the pan. Discard chicken carcass and bay leaf. Add cooked vegetables to the liquid. Cook gently for 5 minutes.

* FRENCH ONION SOUP *

2 kg (4 lb) lean beef, diced
3.8 L (6 pints) cold water
2 brown onions, sliced
½ bunch celery, coarsely
    chopped
salt and freshly ground black
    pepper, to taste
125 g (4 oz) butter
750 g (1½ lb) white onions,
    thinly sliced
melba toast (see glossary)
375 g (12 oz) cheddar cheese,
    freshly grated
parsley, finely chopped, to
    garnish

serves 8

First make beef stock. Place beef in a large saucepan with water. Bring to the boil, then reduce heat, cover saucepan, and simmer for 1 hour.

Cool stock, then put it into the refrigerator until fat sets on top. Remove surface fat and strain. Return stock to saucepan, add brown onions, celery and salt and pepper, and simmer for a further 3 hours. Strain stock, discarding vegetables, and return to a clean pan.

Preheat oven to 180°C (350°F). Melt butter in a saucepan, add white onion, cover and sauté over a low heat until onion is soft and golden. Stir occasionally with a wooden spoon to prevent catching—there must be no hint of burning. Add sautéed onion to stock and simmer for 1 hour.

Cover base of a large baking or casserole dish or with the thinnest possible slices of melba toast. Sprinkle the cheese over the toast. Place in the oven for 10 minutes, or until cheese turns into a deep golden crust.

Pour soup into bowls placing a slice of melba toast carefully on top. Sprinkle with parsley and serve.

* GAZPACHO *

SOUP

1 large tomato, skinned
1 small cucumber, peeled
1 medium-sized green
  capsicum (bell pepper)
125 ml (½ cup) olive oil
60 ml (½ cup) white vinegar
salt and freshly ground black
  pepper, to taste
3 shallots, thinly sliced
1.85 L (7⅓ cups) beef stock
  (see page 378)

GARLIC-FLAVOURED CROUTONS

4 slices white bread
vegetable oil, for frying
2 cloves garlic, crushed
salt

serves 6

To make soup, remove seeds from tomato and cucumber, and cut into 1 cm (½ in) pieces. Remove seeds and pith from green capsicum and cut into 1 cm (½ in) pieces.

In a bowl combine oil, vinegar and salt and pepper to taste. Add tomatoes, cucumber, capsicum and sliced shallots. Allow to stand for 1 hour, stirring occasionally so that vegetables absorb dressing.

To make garlic-flavoured croutons, remove crusts from bread and cut bread into 1 cm (½ in) cubes. Fry cubes in hot oil with garlic until golden. Drain well, and sprinkle with salt before serving.

Strain vegetables well, then add to beef stock, in a large bowl. Chill thoroughly, then serve with garlic-flavoured croutons.

* LEEK, POTATO AND BACON SOUP *

2.5 kg (5 lb) potatoes, peeled
  and cut into chunks
2 leeks, sliced into 3 cm
  (1 in) rings
½ kg (1 lb) bacon, chopped
salt and freshly ground black
  pepper, to taste
1 x 300 g (1¼ cups) sour
  cream
¼ bunch shallots (scallions),
  chopped
½ bunch coriander (cilantro),
  chopped

serves 4–6

Place potatoes in a large saucepan with enough water to cover. Bring water to the boil and cook potatoes for about 10 minutes or until soft. Drain water and save. Mash potatoes with the saved water (adding more water if necessary). The mixture should have the consist-ency of thick soup. Add leek and bacon to the mashed potatoes and simmer until leek is soft and bacon is cooked. Season with salt and pepper.

In a bowl, mix sour cream and shallots. Serve hot, garnished with coriander.

Variations: Add your favourite crispy vegetable a few minutes before serving, add some cream/sour cream to the main body of the soup, or crisply fry the bacon and add it just before serving.

* MINESTRONE *

1 kg (2lb) shin of beef on the
   bone
5 L (20 cups) water
1 large brown onion, sliced
12 black peppercorns
90 g (3 oz) red kidney beans
   (can use tinned)
2 teaspoons salt
1 tablespoon olive oil
2 large tomatoes, skinned and
   quartered
1 stalk celery, sliced
1 carrot, sliced
2 zucchini (courgettes), sliced
1 clove garlic, crushed
125 g (4 oz) bacon, diced
1 tablespoon tomato paste
salt and pepper, to taste
60 g (2 oz) spaghetti or
   macaroni
parmesan cheese, for serving

serves 8

Place beef in a large saucepan with water. Simmer, covered, for 2 hours with onion, peppercorns, kidney beans and salt. Skim surface occasionally to clear soup. Meat should be easily removed from bone when cooking is complete. Cool. Remove surface fat and onion. Discard bones and return meat to stock.

Heat oil in a frying pan and sauté tomatoes, celery, carrot and garlic over a medium heat for 10 minutes. (You may have to add a little more oil.) Transfer vegetables to stock, and add bacon, tomato paste and vegetables. Season with salt and pepper and simmer for 40 minutes.

Add spaghetti 8 minutes before cooking is completed. Sprinkle each serving with grated parmesan cheese and serve.

* OYSTER SOUP *

2.5 L (4 pints) milk
48 oysters, shells removed
465 ml (¾ pint) fish stock
  (see page 382)
90 g (3 oz) butter
pinch of paprika
pinch of celery salt (see
  glossary)
freshly ground black pepper,
  to taste
150 ml (¼ pint) fresh cream
fresh dill or chopped parsley,
  to garnish

serves 8

Scald milk with 12 oysters in a large saucepan. Add fish stock, bring to a gentle simmer then add remaining oysters, butter and paprika. Stir until butter melts. Add celery salt and black pepper. Stir in cream and reheat gently. Serve garnished with a little dill or parsley.

* PEA AND HAM SOUP *

500 g (1 lb) dried split peas
1 kg (2 lb) bacon bones
2.5 L (4 pints) chicken stock
  (see page 380)
2 frankfurters
2 teaspoons white vinegar
sliced sour gherkins, to
  garnish

serves 8

Soak peas overnight. Drain. Add peas and bacon bones to stock, bring to the boil and simmer for 2½ hours. Cool soup and remove bacon bones. Scrape meat off bones and return meat to soup.

Cook frankfurters in boiling water for 3 minutes. Cool frankfurters, then peel them and cut them into 5 mm (¼ in) slices. Add to soup, with white vinegar. Reheat soup and serve with sour gherkins.

* PUMPKIN SOUP *

60 g (2 oz) butter
1 white onion, finely chopped
625 ml (1 pint) chicken stock
  (see page 380)
500 g (1 lb) pumpkin,
  peeled, seeded and cut into
  5 mm (¼ in) chunks
625 ml (1 pint) hot milk
pinch of ground allspice (see
  glossary)
salt and freshly ground black
  pepper, to taste
125 ml (½ cup) thickened
  cream
finely chopped parsley and
  garlic-flavoured croutons
  (see page 27), to garnish

serves 8

Melt butter in a large saucepan and gently fry onion for 10 minutes, or until onion is soft. Add chicken stock and bring to the boil. Add pumpkin to stock and simmer until tender, about 30 minutes. Cool. Purée pumpkin in a food processor or blender. Return soup to pan, add hot milk, allspice, salt and pepper, and heat gently. Add thickened cream just before serving.

Serve in a tureen, lightly sprinkled with parsley and garlic-flavoured croutons.

* SHORT SOUP *

1 egg yolk, beaten
150 g (5 oz) frozen prawns
  (shrimp), thawed and
  chopped
½ cup Chinese cabbage,
  finely chopped
¼ cup onion, finely chopped
1 tablespoon soy sauce
½ teaspoon caster (superfine)
  sugar
¼ teaspoon salt
¼ teaspoon black pepper
¼ teaspoon ground ginger, or
  1 slice fresh ginger, finely
  chopped
20 wonton wrappers (see
  glossary)
2 L (8 cups) chicken stock
  (see page 380)
chopped coriander (cilantro)
  or spring onions (scallions),
  to garnish

serves 6

In a bowl, combine egg yolk, prawns, Chinese cabbage, onion, soy sauce, sugar, salt, pepper and ginger. Mix well and set aside.

Place a wonton wrapper on a flat surface with a point towards you. Spoon a heaped teaspoonful of filling into the centre of skin and fold each point in towards the centre to make a parcel, moistening each corner as you go so that they seal.

Cook wontons in a large saucepan in boiling stock for 3–5 minutes. Serve garnished with chopped coriander or spring onions.

* SCALLOP SOUP *

500 g (1 lb) scallops
125 g (4 oz) butter
625 ml (2½ cups) milk,
   warmed
625 ml (2½ cups) fish stock
   (see page 382)
60 ml (¼ cup) fresh cream
salt and freshly ground black
   pepper, to taste
paprika, chopped spring
   onions (scallions) and
   cracker biscuits, to garnish

serves 4–6

Separate coral from white meat of scallops. Heat butter in a large saucepan until it is bubbling gently, then add scallops and fry for 3 minutes each side, turning over gently. Add milk and fish stock, blending butter in well. Simmer over a low heat for 15 minutes.

In a bowl, blend a little of the hot soup with cream. Stir this back into soup. Season with salt and pepper.

Serve hot, with a sprinkle of paprika and chopped spring onions, accompanied by cracker biscuits. Break biscuits over the soup.

* TOMATO SOUP *

2 rashers bacon, chopped
30 g (1 oz) butter (optional)
2 kg (4 lb) ripe tomatoes,
  skinned and chopped
1 onion, chopped
1 carrot, peeled and grated
1 stick celery, chopped
940 ml (1½ pints) chicken
  stock (see page 380)
salt and black pepper, to taste
bouquet garni (see glossary)

serves 4

Heat bacon in a pan, add butter and melt (if using), then toss in vegetables and cook. Do not allow bacon or onion to brown. Add stock, salt and pepper and bouquet garni, then cover soup and simmer gently for about 35 minutes. Adjust seasoning. Sieve and reheat, then serve.

* TOMATO AND HERB SOUP *

60 g (2 oz) butter
1 tablespoon each of finely
  chopped celery, onion and
  carrot
¼ clove garlic, crushed
2 tablespoons plain (all-
  purpose) flour
1 teaspoon dried mixed herbs
6 black peppercorns
½ bay leaf
1.25 L (2 pints) beef stock
  (see page 378)
500 g (1 lb) tomatoes,
  skinned and chopped
3 cloves
salt and freshly ground black
  pepper, to taste

serves 8

Melt butter in a large saucepan, add celery, onion, carrot and garlic and sauté, covered, over a medium heat, for 5 minutes.

Stir in flour. Add mixed herbs, peppercorns, and bay leaf, then cover and cook gently for a further 5 minutes. Add stock, tomatoes and cloves. Cover and simmer gently for 1 hour. Add salt and pepper and serve.

Variations: Add ½ cup cooked rice, or 30 g (1 oz) tomato paste or ½ cup cooked, chopped ham, during last 10 minutes. For a creamy tomato soup stir in 150 ml (⅔ cup) of cream before serving.

* TOMATO AND TUNA BISQUE *

45 g (1½ oz) butter
1 tablespoon olive oil
1 medium-sized onion, thinly
 sliced
1 clove garlic, crushed
5 tomatoes, sliced
salt and black pepper, to taste
1 tablespoon tomato paste
2 tablespoons plain (all-
 purpose) flour
2 chicken stock cubes
690 ml (2¾ cups) hot water
1 x 205 g (6½ oz) can of
 tuna in brine, drained
125 ml (½ cup) fresh cream
1 tablespoon parsley, chopped

serves 4–6

Melt butter in a saucepan and add oil. Add onion
and garlic and fry until golden brown. Add tomatoes
and salt and pepper and cook gently for 5 minutes, or
until tomato is soft.

Mix tomato paste and flour together in a small
bowl and, when smooth, add to tomato mixture and
combine. Dissolve stock cubes in a little hot water
and gradually stir into tomato mixture.

Bring mixture to the boil, stirring continuously.
Pass soup through a sieve or purée in a food processor
or blender. Add tuna to soup with cream and parsley.
Reheat gently and serve.

Salads

* AVOCADO ORANGE SALAD *

1 mignonette lettuce, washed
  and leaves separated
2 avocados, peeled, stoned
  and sliced
2 oranges, cut into segments
2 tablespoons slivered
  almonds, toasted

Dressing
2 tablespoons orange juice
2 tablespoons olive oil
1 tablespoon white vinegar
1 teaspoon shallots
  (scallions), chopped
¼ teaspoon curry powder
salt and ground black pepper,
  to taste

serves 4

To make dressing, combine ingredients and season to taste.

Line a salad bowl with lettuce leaves. Layer remaining leaves into bowl. Arrange avocados and orange segments decoratively over lettuce. Drizzle dressing onto salad, and sprinkle with almonds.

* BEAN AND BREAD SALAD *

cooking oil spray
12 slices crusty Italian bread
½ teaspoon cracked black
  pepper
½ teaspoon dried oregano
300 g (10 oz) canned borlotti
  beans, drained
12 cherry tomatoes, halved
¼ cup pitted black olives,
  halved
1 small red onion, sliced
¼ cup fresh basil leaves,
  chopped
1 tablespoon balsamic
  vinegar
baby cos lettuce leaves to serve
1 cup fresh basil leaves to
  garnish

serves 4

1 Preheat oven to 180°C/360°F. Lightly spray bread slices on both sides with oil and place on an oven tray. Sprinkle one side of each bread slice with pepper and oregano and bake for 8 minutes, or until lightly browned and crisp.

Combine borlotti beans, tomatoes, olives, red onion, basil and vinegar in a large bowl and mix well. Arrange lettuce leaves on a serving plate with bean mixture and toasted bread. Serve garnished with fresh basil leaves.

* CAESAR SALAD *

1 clove garlic, peeled
1 teaspoon salt
1 teaspoon dry mustard (see
  glossary)
1 tablespoon lemon juice
¼ teaspoon tabasco sauce
3 tablespoons olive oil
1 cos lettuce, leaves washed
  and dried
1 endive, leaves washed and
  dried
2 tablespoons parmesan
  cheese, grated
4 anchovy fillets, chopped
  into 3–4 pieces
1 coddled egg (boiled for
  1 minute)
garlic-flavoured croutons
  (see page 27)

serves 6–8

Rub salad bowl with cut clove of garlic. Put salt, mustard, lemon juice and tabasco sauce into bowl and stir with wooden spoon until salt dissolves. Add olive oil and blend well.

Tear salad greens into bite-sized pieces and place in salad bowl. Sprinkle with grated cheese and add anchovy fillets. Break in the coddled egg and toss well, until all ingredients are well coated with dressing.

Just before serving, sprinkle with garlic-flavoured croutons and toss again.

* CALAMARI SALAD WITH BASIL DRESSING *

300 g (10 oz) calamari
   tubes, washed and sliced
   into 1 cm (½ in) rings
250 ml (1 cup) water
80 ml (⅓ cup) lemon juice
80 ml (⅓ cup) grapeseed oil
   (see glossary)
150 g (5 oz) snow peas,
   trimmed
100 g (3½ oz) button
   mushrooms
1 punnet cherry tomatoes
1 green capsicum (bell
   pepper), seeds and pith
   removed and cut into strips
2 tablespoons chives, chopped

Basil Dressing
60 ml (¼ cup) French
   dressing (see page 356)
½ cup chopped fresh basil

serves 2

Cook calamari in simmering water for 2 minutes or until cooked. Drain.

Combine lemon juice and grapeseed oil. Pour mixture into a bowl and add calamari. Toss calamari until coated. Cover bowl with cling wrap and refrigerate overnight.

Place snow peas, mushrooms, tomatoes, capsicum and chives into a salad bowl.

Drain calamari, reserving marinade. Add calamari to salad and chill for 30 minutes, covered. In a bowl or jar, combine dressing ingredients and reserved marinade. Chill for 30 minutes.

Just before serving, drizzle dressing over salad and toss lightly.

* CHINESE EGG NOODLES SALAD WITH CHICKEN *

1 double breast of chicken,
  thinly sliced
1 tablespoon sesame oil
½ Chinese cabbage, sliced
½ cup slivered almonds
100 g (3½ oz) chinese fried
  egg noodles, cooked
4 spring onions (scallions),
  finely chopped
2 tomatoes, finely chopped

Dressing
125 ml (½ cup) olive oil
125 ml (½ cup) balsamic
  vinegar
60 g (2 oz) caster (superfine)
  sugar
pinch of salt
2 tablespoons soy sauce

serves 6–8

Heat oil in a frying pan and fry chicken. Set aside to cool.

To make dressing, combine all ingredients in a bowl (or jar) and mix well (or put the lid on and shake).

To serve, place chicken, Chinese cabbage, almonds, egg noodles, shallots and tomatoes in a bowl. Toss to combine, pour over dressing and serve immediately.

* COLESLAW *

½ small cabbage, shredded
2 carrots, grated
1 onion, grated
1 clove garlic, crushed
   (optional)
⅔ stalk celery, sliced
2 tablespoons olive oil
125 ml (½ cup) mayonnaise
   (see page 364)
1 teaspoon salt
freshly ground black pepper,
   to taste
pinch of caster (superfine)
   sugar

serves 4–6

Mix cabbage, carrots, onion, garlic and celery in a large salad bowl.

Combine olive oil, mayonnaise, salt and pepper and sugar in a separate bowl. Stir dressing through salad and serve immediately.

* CRAB SALAD *

400 g (14 oz) crabmeat, fresh or canned
4 crisp celery sticks, finely chopped
½ cup French dressing (see page 356)
salt and freshly ground black pepper, to taste
4 small butter lettuces, shredded
4 sprigs chives, to garnish

serves 4

In a mixing bowl, combine crabmeat and celery. Moisten with French dressing and salt and pepper and mix well.

Line a salad bowl with the shredded lettuce. Pile the crab on top.

Add some more dressing, scatter with chives just before serving.

* CUCUMBER SALAD *

3 cucumbers, washed, dried
  and thinly sliced
1 tablespoon salt
2 cloves garlic, cut into
  slivers
180 ml (¾ cup) balsamic
  vinegar
2 tablespoons sugar
freshly ground white pepper
1 tablespoon parsley,
  chopped, or fresh dill, to
  garnish

serves 6–8

Arrange cucumber slices in a deep bowl and sprinkle with salt. Cover with a small plate that fits inside the bowl and place a heavy weight on top. Let this stand at room temperature for 2 hours.

Place garlic slivers in vinegar and let stand for at least 30 minutes.

Drain away juice from cucumber completely; squeeze cucumber as dry as possible. Add sugar and pepper to garlic-flavoured vinegar and pour over cucumber. Taste and adjust seasonings if necessary. Cover tightly and chill thoroughly.

Before serving, drain off vinegar and sprinkle cucumber salad with chopped parsley or dill.

* LAMB SALAD *

¾ cup cracked wheat (see glossary)
185 ml (1¼ cups) hot water
1 teaspoon butter
½ teaspoon ground tarragon
1 chicken stock cube, crumbled
½ teaspoon curry powder
1½ teaspoons dry mustard (see glossary)
½ teaspoon cayenne pepper
250 g (½ lb) cooked lamb, diced
1 onion, finely chopped
½ cup celery, sliced
2 tablespoons natural yoghurt
2 tablespoons mayonnaise (see page 364)
lettuce cups, for serving
2 hard-boiled eggs, sliced, to garnish
parsley sprigs, to garnish

serves 4–6

Combine wheat, water, butter, ground tarragon, stock cube, curry powder, dry mustard and cayenne in a saucepan and heat, stirring, until the mixture boils. Reduce heat, cover, and simmer for 10 minutes, or until all liquid is absorbed. Cool.

Add lamb, onion, celery, yoghurt and mayonnaise, and toss well. Chill for 30 minutes before serving.

To serve, spoon salad into lettuce cups, and garnish with egg slices and parsley.

* LAMB WITH SESAME SEEDS SALAD *

60 ml (¼ cup) sesame oil
2 cloves garlic, finely chopped
200 g (6½ oz) lamb loin,
  seasoned with salt and
  freshly ground black pepper
mixed lettuce leaves
50 g (1⅔ oz) sesame seeds
freshly ground black pepper,
  to taste
100 ml (⅖ cup) lamb or veal
  stock
4 teaspoons sherry vinegar
  (see glossary)

serves 2

In a heavy frying pan, heat oil and sauté garlic and seasoned lamb. Cook to your taste. Remove lamb from pan and slice into strips.

To serve, place lettuce on serving dish, top with lamb strips and sprinkle over sesame seeds and pepper. Deglaze pan with stock and vinegar and pour sauce over salad.

* LOBSTER SALAD *

2 medium-sized lobsters,
  cooked
4 lettuce cups
150 ml (⅔ cup) mayonnaise
  (see page 364)
2 lemons, juiced
2 tomatoes, sliced
½ avocados, sliced
parsley, finely chopped

serves 4

Crack the lobster claws with a light weight. If you
have special lobster picks, leave the meat in the
cracked shells, otherwise carefully take out the meat
with a fine skewer. If leaving the meat in the claws,
arrange these beside the body of the lobster. Remove
meat from the shell, dice and place back in the shell.
If removing the meat from the claws, blend it with
the body meat.

   Arrange lobster on lettuce, and top with some
mayonnaise. Mix together the lemon juice, tomatoes,
avocado and parsley and serve on the side.

* MEDITERRANEAN CHICKEN PASTA SALAD *

1.5 kg (3 lb) chicken thighs
200 g (6½ oz) pasta twirls
100 g (3½ oz) pesto (see glossary)
200 g (6½ oz) sun-dried tomatoes in oil, sliced
200 g (6½ oz) snow peas, blanched and sliced
10 small mushrooms, sliced
¼ stick of celery, sliced
2 tablespoons balsamic vinegar
salt and freshly ground black pepper, to taste
1 lettuce (use your favourite variety), washed and leaves torn

serves 6

Boil the chicken, and allow to cool. De-bone and cut up into bite-sized pieces.

Boil pasta for 8 minutes (in chicken stock if you wish, but it makes little difference to the dish), then rinse in cool water and drain. While pasta is warm, stir in pesto and sun-dried tomatoes and their oil.

Stir snow peas, mushrooms and celery into pasta, then add chicken. Sprinkle over balsamic vinegar and stir in, then season with salt and pepper. Let the dish sit for a few hours in the refrigerator, if possible.

When serving, put a layer of leaves on each plate first, then top with the chicken and pasta mix.

Note: You can use a mixture of types of lettuce (or other succulent leaves), which will improve the look and taste of the dish by giving it a range of colours, shapes and flavours. You can also add capsicum, or other mild herbs, but try to avoid strong flavours, such as onions or shallots.

* PASTA SALAD *

500 g (1 lb) cooked spiral
  noodles
1 tablespoon olive oil
½ teaspoon salt
½ red capsicum (bell pepper),
  seeds and pith removed and
  diced
4–6 mushrooms, sliced
4–6 shallots (scallions),
  finely chopped
125 g (4 oz) mung beans
125 g (4 oz) corn kernels
  (optional)
300 ml (10½ fl oz)
  mayonnaise (see page 364)

serves 6–8

Place pasta into a large saucepan of boiling water
with oil and salt, and cook for 8 minutes or until
pasta is al dente. Rinse and strain.

Place all ingredients except dressing in a bowl and
toss to combine. Add dressing to taste.

* POTATO SALAD *

1 kg (2 lb) potatoes, peeled
75 ml (⅓ cup) French
  dressing (see page 356)
½ cup cucumber, finely
  chopped
½ cup celery, finely chopped
¼ cup onion, finely sliced
4 hard-boiled eggs, coarsely
  chopped
250 ml (1 cup) mayonnaise
  (see page 364)
125 g (½ cup) sour cream
1 tablespoon horseradish
  relish
salt and freshly ground black
  pepper, to taste
2 rashers bacon, cooked and
  finely chopped, to garnish

serves 6–8

Cook potatoes in boiling salted water until just tender. Drain well and leave to cool just enough to be handled, then cut into small cubes.

Place potato in a bowl and pour over French dressing, while potatoes are still warm. Let potatoes cool, then add cucumber, celery, onion and egg.

In a bowl, combine mayonnaise, sour cream and horseradish relish. Pour over potatoes and toss gently. Season with salt and pepper.

Garnish with bacon just before serving.

* SEAFOOD SALAD *

1 small crayfish or 500 g
  (1 lb) prawns, shelled,
  deveined and cooked
12 scallops, poached in white
  wine (see page 176) and
  drained
250 g (8 oz) bream fillets,
  poached and flaked
250 g (1 cup) French
  dressing (see page 356)
1 tablespoon lemon juice
250 g (1 cup) sour cream or
  mayonnaise (see page 364)
125 ml (½ cup) tomato
  ketchup
1 cup celery, finely sliced
1 head lettuce, washed and
  finely shredded
12–16 plump oysters, chilled
parsley, chopped, to garnish

serves 6

Remove flesh from crayfish body and legs, and cut into cubes. In a bowl, combine crayfish or prawns, scallops and bream. Pour French dressing and lemon juice over seafood, then cover bowl and marinate for 1 hour in the refrigerator.

Drain excess French dressing. In a small bowl, mix sour cream with tomato ketchup and celery and fold through seafood.

Spoon seafood and sauce on a bed of finely shredded lettuce in chilled individual bowls. Top with chilled oysters and sprinkle with finely chopped parsley.

* SPANISH POTATO SALAD *

1 tablespoon olive oil
1 tablespoon vinegar
salt and freshly ground black
  pepper, to taste
2 cups hot cooked potatoes,
  diced
125 g (4 oz) black olives or
  green and black combined
2 hard-boiled eggs
1 cup celery, sliced or
  cucumber, diced
¼ cup pickled cucumber,
  diced
¼ cup green capsicum (bell
  pepper), seeds and pith
  removed and diced
80 g (⅓ cup) mayonnaise
  (see page 364)
1 teaspoon onion, chopped

serves 6–8

In a screw-top jar or small bowl, blend oil, vinegar, salt and pepper. Pour over hot potatoes, toss lightly and allow to cool.

Cut olives into quarters. Cut eggs lengthwise and slice horizontally.

Combine cooled potatoes, olives, eggs, celery, pickled cucumber and green capsicum. In a cup, blend mayonnaise and onion. Mix this lightly into salad. Chill well before serving.

* THAI BEEF SALAD *

6 lettuce leaves
500 g (1 lb) beef rump or
  tenderloin, roasted and
  sliced into strips
2 cloves garlic, finely chopped
1 Spanish onion, sliced
1 stalk lemongrass
¼ cup coriander leaves, torn
1 cup mint leaves, torn
fried onion, to garnish
1 tablespoon dried chilli
  flakes, to garnish

Dressing
4 kaffir lime leaves, cut into
  strips
3 cloves garlic, finely chopped
5 green serrano chillies,
  seeded and finely chopped
1 tablespoon fish sauce
juice of 1 lime
¼ cup palm sugar or brown
  sugar

serves 6

To make the salad dressing, combine all ingredients in a bowl (or jar) and mix well (or put lid on and shake).

To serve, arrange lettuce leaves on a serving dish, covering the whole surface area. Place strips of beef over lettuce and sprinkle over garlic, onion, lemongrass, coriander and mint.

Pour the dressing over the top and garnish with fried onion and chilli flakes.

* WALDORF SALAD *

1 green apple
1 red apple
juice of ½ lemon
1 cup celery, finely chopped
½ cup walnuts, chopped
60 g (¼ cup) mayonnaise
   (see page 364)
crisp lettuce cups
1 red apple, thinly sliced,
   brushed with lemon juice
   to prevent discolouration,
   to garnish

serves 6–8

Chill apples, then core and dice them. Pour lemon juice over apples. Add celery, walnuts and mayonnaise and combine.

Serve piled into lettuce cups and garnish with slices of red apple.

Light meals & snacks

* BACON-WRAPPED SHRIMP *

500 g (1 lb) green prawns
  (shrimp), peeled and
  deveined
6–8 rashers bacon, rind
  removed and rashers halved
bamboo skewers, soaked in
  water
60 g (2 oz) butter, melted
60 ml (¼ cup) lemon juice

serves 6

Wrap each prawn in a piece of bacon and thread onto
bamboo skewers. In a small bowl or jug, combine
melted butter and lemon juice. Brush over kebabs.

Barbecue kebabs over hot coals for approximately
10–15 minutes, or until prawns are cooked and bacon
is lightly brown and crisp. Turn frequently while
cooking, and brush again with the melted butter
and lemon juice before serving. Serve any remaining
butter with the kebabs.

* BAKED POTATOES *

4 *medium potatoes*
1 *head of garlic*
2 *rosemary sprigs*

serves 4

Preheat oven to 200°C (400°F). Scrub potatoes under running water and prick once with a skewer or a fork. Add the head of garlic and the rosemary. This stops them exploding in the oven. Put potatoes at the back of the centre shelf in the oven and bake for 1½ hours.

Remove potatoes from the oven and, using oven gloves, immediately break them in half. If you leave them whole, the skin goes wrinkly and soft.

Serve with butter or sour cream.

Note: Do not turn the oven down at all while the potatoes are cooking—they will go soft immediately.

* BARBECUED CHICKEN DRUMSTICKS *

12 chicken drumsticks

Marinade
60 ml (¼ cup) tomato sauce
2–3 tablespoons lemon juice
2 tablespoons soy sauce
60 ml (¼ cup) olive oil
½ teaspoon salt

serves 6

Barbecue chicken drumsticks over medium coals, turning frequently and basting with the marinade while cooking. Cook until drumsticks are tender.

To make the marinade, combine marinade ingredients in a large bowl and mix together well. Put chicken drumsticks into the bowl, cover and

* BARBECUED SPARE RIBS *

1 clove garlic, crushed
salt and black pepper, to taste
pinch of salt
1 tablespoon brown sugar
1 teaspoon paprika
1 teaspoon dry mustard (see
    glossary)
8 pork spareribs
barbecue sauce, for serving

serves 8

In a bowl, combine garlic, salt and pepper, salt, sugar, paprika and mustard. Rub spareribs with this seasoning.

Barbecue spareribs over medium coals, turning frequently and basting with the barbecue sauce while cooking. Cook for 15–20 minutes, or until spareribs are tender.

Serve with baked potatoes and coleslaw (see page 56).

* BOILED EGGS *

2 eggs

serves 1

Place eggs in boiling water for 3 minutes for soft-boiled eggs and 6 minutes for hard-boiled eggs. Put eggs into cold water after cooking to cool slightly. This helps to remove shell easily.

* CRUMBED CALAMARI RINGS *

750 g (1½ lb) squid tubes
   (squid hoods)
260 g (9 oz) plain (all-
   purpose) flour
sea salt and pepper
2–3 eggs
260 ml (9 fl oz) milk
olive oil, for deep-frying
lemon wedges, to serve

serves 6

Cut squid tubes into 5 mm (¼ inch) rings. Place the rings on absorbent paper and dry well.

Sift plain flour into a bowl and season with salt and pepper.

Whisk eggs and milk together in a shallow bowl.

Toss the squid rings into the flour, one at a time, then dip into the milk mixture, shaking off any extra liquid.

Heat oil to smoking point (it may spit and splatter, so be careful). Cook the rings in the hot oil until lightly golden (3 minutes maximum). Drain well and serve hot with lemon wedges.

* CHARCOAL-GRILLED SHRIMP *

1 kg (2 lb) green prawns
(shrimp), peeled and
deveined

Marinade
250 ml (1 cup) olive oil
60 ml (¼ cup) lemon juice
½ cup onion, finely chopped
2 cloves garlic, crushed
¼ cup parsley, finely chopped

serves 4

To make marinade, place all marinade ingredients in a large bowl and mix well. Add prawns to the bowl and combine. Cover bowl and let stand for several hours in the refrigerator. Drain prawns.

Place prawns in a heavy-based frying pan or skillet and cook over medium coals for 10–15 minutes, or until cooked. Stir frequently and add a little marinade while cooking. Serve immediately.

* CHEESE SOUFFLÉ *

60 g (2 oz) butter
1 tablespoon fresh white
  breadcrumbs
75 g (2½ oz) parmesan
  cheese, grated
3 tablespoons plain (all-
  purpose) flour
280 ml (9 fl oz) milk
4 egg yolks
¾ teaspoon salt
¼ teaspoon ground black
  pepper
pinch of cayenne pepper
¼ teaspoon paprika
30 g (1 oz) gruyère cheese,
  grated
5 egg whites

serves 4

Preheat oven to 200°C (400°F). Grease the inside of a 15 cm (6 in) soufflé dish with 15 g (½ oz) butter, then sprinkle with breadcrumbs and 1 tablespoon parmesan cheese. Cut a band of greaseproof paper about 18 cm (7 in) wide (it needs to stick up 5 cm (2 in) higher than the top of the dish), and long enough to go round the outside of the dish. Fold the paper in half lengthways and butter the top half of one side of it. Tie the paper round the soufflé dish with string, with the butter side on the inside, sticking up beyond the dish.

Melt remaining butter in a saucepan, stir in flour and cook over a gentle heat for about 1 minute. Add milk and stir continuously over a moderate heat until mixture thickens and boils. Simmer for 5 seconds. Remove from heat, add egg yolks one at a time, beating in well. Add seasonings, remaining parmesan cheese and gruyere cheese.

Whisk egg whites until they form stiff, firm peaks. Stir a heaped tablespoon of egg white into the sauce to lighten it, then gently fold in the remaining egg whites. Pour soufflé mixture into soufflé dish. Bake on middle shelf of the oven for 30–40 minutes. Serve immediately.

* CHICKEN SATAY STICKS *

185 g (6 oz) chicken
few drops soy sauce
few drops of tabasco sauce
1 teaspoon white vinegar
1 teaspoon oil
1 teaspoon brown sugar
1 clove garlic
bamboo skewers, soaked in
    water

serves 2

Cut chicken into 1.25 cm (½ in) cubes, leaving the fat on. In a bowl, combine soy sauce, tabasco sauce, white vinegar, oil, brown sugar and garlic. Put chicken cubes into bowl and marinate for at least 2 hours in the refrigerator.

Put chicken cubes on skewers and grill very quickly under a hot grill. Serve on the skewers accompanied by a bed of rice.

* CINNAMON TOAST *

125 g (4 oz) caster
    (superfine) sugar
2–3 teaspoons ground
    cinnamon
6 slices white bread
butter, softened

serves 3

Mix sugar and cinnamon in a bowl.

Toast the bread lightly on both sides and butter one side, spreading the butter right to the edges. Using a spoon, sprinkle each slice of toast evenly with the cinnamon and sugar mixture. Put the toast under the grill and cook until the sugar starts to melt. Remove and serve hot.

* LAMB KEBABS *

1 x 2 kg (4 lb) leg of lamb
500 g (1 lb) small onions
1 green capsicum (bell
  pepper), pith and seeds
  removed
2 rashers bacon
6–12 button mushrooms
6 bamboo skewers
6 small tomatoes
bay leaves (optional)
salt and freshly ground black
  pepper, to taste
olive oil or melted butter

serves 6

Soak the bamboo skewers in water for 10 minutes prior to use.

Cut lamb into 2.5 cm (1 in) cubes. Peel onions and blanch in boiling water, then drain. Cut capsicum and bacon into 2.5 cm (1 in) pieces.

Thread lamb onto skewers alternately with onion, mushrooms, capsicum, bacon and tomatoes. Small bay leaves can be added if used. Season with salt and pepper and brush with oil. Grill gently, turning and brushing again with oil if necessary, for 20–25 minutes, or until meat is cooked.

Serve on a bed of fried rice.

* CORN ON THE COB *

4 corn on the cob
30 g (1 oz) butter
salt and freshly ground black
  pepper, to taste

serves 4

Turn back husks of the corn and strip off silk. Brush corn with melted butter or margarine and sprinkle with salt and freshly ground black pepper. Replace the husks and secure in three places with string.

Barbecue corn cobs over hot coals for 15–20 minutes, or until tender, turning frequently. When cooked, husks will be dry and brown and corn will be golden brown. Serve with melted butter and salt and pepper.

Variation: After stripping off silk, wrap a bacon rasher (remove rind first) around each corn cob and secure at the ends with cocktail sticks. Replace the husks and proceed as above.
Note: Select young, tender corn cobs by checking they are a bright yellow in colour and not wrinkled. You can remove husks from corn cobs completely. If you do this, brush corn with melted butter and season with salt and pepper, then wrap each corn cob in aluminium foil and barbecue over hot coals for 20 minutes, or until tender. Serve as above.

* CRUMBED LAMB CUTLETS *

8 lamb cutlets
lemon juice, to taste
  (optional)
salt and freshly ground black
  pepper, to taste
plain (all-purpose) flour, for
  coating
1 egg, beaten with
  1 tablespoon of water
breadcrumbs, for coating
olive oil, for frying
parsley, chopped, to garnish

serves 4

Trim skin and excess fat from cutlets and flatten with the side of a meat mallet (unless your butcher has already done this). Lay cutlets on a plate, sprinkle with a little lemon juice (if using) and season with salt and pepper. Let cutlets stand in refrigerator for 1 hour. To finish cutlets, coat with flour then dip in beaten egg and finally breadcrumbs, pressing them on firmly.

Pour enough oil to be 5 mm (¼ in) deep in a heavy frying pan and heat. Fry cutlets over a moderate heat for 4–5 minutes on either side, then lift them out and drain them on absorbent paper.

Serve immediately, while still crisp and piping hot, garnished with parsley.

Variations:
Parsley Cutlets: to each 30 g (1 oz) breadcrumbs, add 2 tablespoons finely chopped parsley.
Parmesan Cutlets: to each 30 g (1 oz) breadcrumbs, add 2 tablespoons grated parmesan cheese.
Rosemary Cutlets: to each 30 g (1 oz) breadcrumbs add ¼ teaspoon powdered or ½ teaspoon dried spikes of rosemary.

* DOLMADES (STUFFED VINE LEAVES) *

16 fresh or tinned vine leaves
  (see glossary)
500 g (1 lb) lean minced
  (ground) beef
220 g (7 oz) long grain rice
2 onions, finely chopped
1 clove garlic, crushed
2 teaspoons salt
½ teaspoon freshly ground
  black pepper
1 teaspoon dried oregano
  leaves
1 tablespoon fresh mint,
  chopped
625 ml (2½ cups) beef stock
  (see page 378)

serves 4

If using fresh vine leaves, choose medium-sized leaves that are not too dark in colour. Large, dark leaves are tough. Snip off stems with kitchen scissors, wash well, place in a bowl and pour boiling water over to soften. If using tinned vine leaves in brine, wash in warm water before filling.

To prepare meat filling, combine all remaining ingredients except stock in a bowl, mixing thoroughly. Divide mixture into 16 portions and shape into small sausage shapes. On a wooden board, arrange one leaf at a time, shiny side down, and place a portion of filling on the leaf, near the stem. Fold over top of leaf, then sides. Roll up, enclosing meat completely.

Pack rolls close together, in neat rows, in a heavy saucepan. If necessary, put a second layer on top of the first. Pour stock into the saucepan and cover with lid. Bring slowly to a simmer and cook gently for 45 minutes to 1 hour. Serve hot.

✳ FISHCAKES ✳

250 g (8 oz) white fish,
  poached or steamed
250 g (8 oz) mashed potatoes
1 egg
salt and freshly ground black
  pepper, to taste
30–60 g (1–2 oz) butter for
  frying
parsley and lemon, to garnish

Coating
15–30 g (½–1 oz) seasoned
  flour (see glossary)
1 egg, beaten
3–4 tablespoons crisp
  breadcrumbs

serves 4

Remove all bones and skin from the fish, then flake with a fork. In a bowl, place fish, potato, egg and seasoning. Mix well, then divide into 8 round cakes.

Coat the fishcakes in seasoned flour, then egg, then breadcrumbs.

Heat butter in a frying pan and fry fishcakes for 2–3 minutes, until golden brown on the underside. Turn, then cook for the same time on the second side. Lift out of pan and drain on absorbent paper.

Serve hot, garnished with lemon.

* FRENCH TOAST *

3–4 eggs
125 ml (½ cup) milk
2 tablespoons caster
   (superfine) sugar
¼ teaspoon vanilla essence
pinch of salt
butter, for frying
8 thick slices of bread

serves 4

In a large bowl, combine eggs, milk, sugar, vanilla and salt.

Heat a little butter in a frying pan over medium heat. Dip a slice of bread into the egg mixture until bread is completely coated and has soaked up some egg mixture. Place bread in the frying pan and cook for 1 minute on each side, or until it is crisp and golden. Repeat with remaining bread, until egg mixture has all been used.

Serve hot with maple syrup, bacon and fried or raw banana.

* FRIED EGGS *

2 eggs
1 tablespoon olive oil,
   for frying

serves 1

Warm frying pan, adding oil to cover the surface. Put egg rings in the frying pan and crack eggs into them. Cook on a low heat for 2 minutes for sunny side up; flip eggs and cook for another minute if you prefer easy over eggs.

Serve hot with buttered toast.

* FRIED ONION AND POTATO BALLS *

4 large potatoes, washed and
 peeled
1 onion, chopped
1 tablespoon butter
60 g (2 oz) plain (all-
 purpose) wholemeal flour
salt and freshly ground black
 pepper, to taste
dash of milk
125 ml (½ cup) vegetable oil

serves 4

Cook potatoes in boiling salted water until tender.
Drain and place in a bowl.

Fry onion in butter until soft and golden.

Mash potatoes, then add flour, salt and pepper,
fried onion and just enough milk to form a firm
dough. Roll into small balls about 2.5 cm (1 in) in
size.

Heat oil in a large frying pan and fry onion and
potato balls until golden brown all over. Drain on
absorbent paper and serve with a green salad.

* FRIED OYSTERS *

12 oysters
salt and freshly ground black
 pepper, to taste
1 egg yolk
60 ml (¼ cup) milk
breadcrumbs, to coat
olive oil, for frying
chopped parsley, to garnish
lemon wedges

serves 1–2

Remove oysters from shell and season with salt and
pepper. Set shells aside.

In a bowl, whisk egg yolk with milk. Dip oysters in
mixture, drain, then roll in breadcrumbs. Deep-fry in
hot oil for 2 minutes. Warm shells in oven and place
fried oysters in them.

* FRIED SHRIMP *

2 shallots (scallions), finely
  chopped
3 slices fresh ginger
2 tablespoons dry sherry
1 teaspoon salt
1 tablespoon cornflour
  (cornstarch)
1 kg (2 lb) green prawns
  (shrimp), peeled and
  deveined
olive oil, for frying

serves 4

In a bowl, combine shallots, ginger, sherry, salt and
cornflour, and mix until smooth. Coat prawns with
the mixture.

  In a large frying pan, heat oil until hot and fry
prawns for 3–5 minutes, depending on their size.
You'll know the prawns are cooked when their meat
turns white. Serve immediately.

* FRIED SCALLOPS *

500 g (1 lb) scallops
flour seasoned with salt and
  black pepper (see glossary)
batter (see page 344)
pinch of paprika
olive oil, for frying
parsley sprigs, to garnish

serves 4

Roll scallops in seasoned flour, dip in batter and
sprinkle with paprika . Deep-fry in hot oil for 1
minute, or until batter is golden. Drain scallops on
paper towelling.

  Fry parsley sprigs in hot oil until crisp. Drain and
serve with french fries (see page 114) and a green
salad.

* GARLIC BREAD *

1 French bread
2 cloves garlic, peeled and
  crushed
250 g (8 oz) butter

serves 4

Preheat oven to 220°C (420°F). With a sharp knife, cut bread into slices almost to the bottom, being careful not to sever the slices.

In a small bowl, mash garlic thoroughly into butter. Spread garlic butter generously on both sides of bread slices. Wrap bread loosely in aluminium foil, place in the oven for 10–15 minutes, and bake until bread is crisp and golden. Serve hot.

* GARLIC SHRIMP *

125 ml (½ cup) olive oil
4 large cloves garlic, peeled
1 tablespoon parsley, chopped
½ teaspoon salt
1 kg (2 lb) small green
  prawns (shrimp), peeled
  and deveined

**serves 12 as an appetiser,
8 as an entrée**

In a bowl, combine oil, garlic, parsley and salt. Add prawns and let stand for 2 hours covered in the refrigerator.

Preheat oven to 250°C (485°F). Place prawns and marinade in an ovenproof casserole dish and cook in the oven for 10 minutes, or until prawns turn pink. Remove garlic cloves.

Serve as an appetiser on small cocktail sticks, or as an entrée in small ramekins.

* GLAZED ONIONS *

500 g (1 lb) small onions
30 g (1 oz) butter
1 teaspoon brown sugar
salt and freshly ground black
  pepper, to taste

serves 4

Peel onions and blanch for 5–7 minutes. Drain well. Put into a saucepan with butter, sugar and seasoning. Cook gently with lid on, shaking and stirring from time to time, until onions become tender and well glazed. This should take 7–10 minutes. Make sure that the cooking is slow, or the sugar will burn. Serve hot.

* GRILLED LAMB CUTLETS *

2 double lamb cutlets
salt and freshly ground black
  pepper, to taste
olive oil for frying

serves 2

Trim cutlets of excess fat and season well on each side. Put on rack in grill pan, and brush with oil. Cook under a very hot grill for 2 minutes to sear meat. Turn and sear other side for 2 minutes. Move the grill pan down and cook for a further 10 minutes (turning once after 5 minutes), or until cooked. Serve with glazed carrots, spinach and mashed potatoes (see page 111).

* GUACAMOLE *

2 tablespoons lemon juice
2–3 tablespoons olive oil
½ clove garlic, peeled and
   crushed
salt, to taste
½ teaspoon tabasco sauce
1 large avocado, diced
2 heaped tablespoons sour
   cream
1 small onion, finely chopped
1 tomato, diced

serves 8

Place all ingredients except onion and tomato in a bowl and beat together with a fork until a smooth consistency is reached. Add tomato and onion and mix through. Serve with corn chips.

* HAM AND PINEAPPLE PIZZA *

1 round piece Lebanese bread
3 tablespoons Italian tomato
  sauce (see page 362) or
  tomato paste
125 g (4 oz) mozzarella
  cheese, grated

**Ham and pineapple
topping**
100 g (3½ oz) sliced ham
1 x 440 g (14 oz) can
  crushed pineapple

serves 2

Preheat oven to 200°C (400°F). Place the bread on a pizza plate or baking sheet. Using a knife, spread the bread very thinly with the tomato sauce or tomato paste. Sprinkle with half the cheese. This is the basic pizza base.

Cut ham slices into pieces about 1 cm (½ in) square. Open the can of pine-apple and drain off juice. Place ham slices on top of the cheese, then add pineapple pieces. Cover with the rest of the cheese.

Cook in the oven until the cheese turns golden brown (about 10 minutes) and serve.

* MASHED POTATO *

4 medium-sized potatoes,
  peeled
125 ml (½ cup) milk
30 g (1 oz)
60 g (2 oz) cheese, grated
salt and freshly ground black
  pepper, to taste

serves 4

Place potatoes into a saucepan with cold, lightly salted water to cover. Bring to the boil and cook gently, covered, for 20–30 minutes, until potatoes are easily pierced with a fork. Drain thoroughly, then shake pan over heat for a minute or two until all surplus moisture has evaporated and potatoes are dry.

Mash potatoes, then beat with a wooden spoon until very smooth. In a saucepan, heat milk and butter. Once mixture is hot, add potatoes and beat until light and fluffy. Add cheese and stir through until melted. Season with salt and pepper. Serve immediately.

* HAMBURGERS *

1 small onion, grated
500 g (1 lb) minced steak
3 tablespoons plain (all-
    purpose) flour
60 ml (¼ cup) milk
125 g (4 oz) extra plain (all-
    purpose) flour
60 ml (¼ cup) oil
6 hamburger buns

serves 6

Mix onion and meat thoroughly in a bowl using a wooden spoon. Add flour and mix in thoroughly. Pour milk over meat mixture and stir in well.

Place extra flour in a small bowl. Make a heaped tablespoon of the meat mixture into a ball and roll it in the flour until it is well coated. Lift it out onto a plate and flatten it slightly. Continue until all the meat is used.

Pour oil into a frying pan and place over a medium heat. When the oil starts to bubble, gently place hamburger patties in the pan. Cook until the bottom of the hamburgers are brown, then flip them over and cook until they are brown on the other side. Drain patties on absorbent paper. (They can also be grilled or barbecued.)

Place patties on hamburger buns and add tomato sauce, sliced cheese,sliced cucumber, sliced tomatoes, sliced beetroot and lettuce—or salad ingredients of your choice.

* FRENCH FRIES*

6 large potatoes
300 ml (10½ fl oz) vegetable
  oil, for deep-frying
salt, to taste

serves 2

Peel potatoes and cut into pieces 5 x 1 x 1 cm (2 x ½ x ½ in). Place in a large bowl and cover with ice cold water for at least 30 minutes. Dry french fries thoroughly in a clean tea towel.

Heat oil until very hot—a 2.5 cm (1 in) cube of bread will brown in 1 minutes when the oil is hot enough. Place dry fries in a frying basket and lower into the oil. The fries should be completely covered by oil. Fry until tender but not browne, for about 10 minutes. Remove fries from oil and drain. Put chips aside until just before serving time.

Reheat oil and cook fries until golden, crisp and slightly puffy. Drain very well, sprinkle with salt, and serve immediately.

Variation: For potato straws, cut potatoes into matchstick-shaped pieces, then prepare and fry as above.

* MEAT PIE *

2 tablespoons oil

1 kg (2 lb) chuck or skirt
  steak, cut into 2.5 cm
  (1 in) cubes

2 onions, chopped

½ cup celery, chopped

½ cup carrot, chopped

500 ml (2 cups) beef stock
  (see page 378)

2 teaspoons salt

¼ teaspoon freshly ground
  black pepper

¼ teaspoon ground nutmeg

3 tablespoons plain (all-
  purpose) flour

185 g (6 oz) short crust
  pastry (see page 345)

beaten egg, for glazing

serves 8

Heat oil in a large saucepan and fry steak in about three lots until browned, then remove. Add onion, celery and carrot and cook for a few minutes. Replace meat, add stock, cover and simmer gently for 1 hour. Add salt, pepper and nutmeg and simmer for another hour, until cooked.

In a cup, blend flour with a little cold water to form a smooth paste. Add to saucepan and cook a little longer, until mixture thickens. Taste and adjust flavour.

Preheat oven to 200°C (400°F). Place a pie funnel in the centre of a large pie dish, then add meat to come to within 2 cm (1 in) of the top.

Roll out pastry on a lightly floured board, so that it is 2.5 cm (1 in) larger than the top of the pie dish. Cut a strip 1 cm (½ in) wide off the edge and place it on the dampened edge of the pie dish. Glaze this strip of pastry with egg, then lift remaining pastry on, easing it gently. (If you stretch it, it will shrink during cooking.) Press edges together, then trim combined edge and decorate with a knife. Glaze pastry with egg. Make a few holes in the pastry for steam to escape. Bake in the oven for 25 minutes, or until cooked.

* MUSSELS WITH GARLIC *

72 mussels in their shells,
   washed
1 L (4 cups) water
250 g (8 oz) butter
salt and freshly ground black
   pepper, to taste
2 cloves garlic, finely chopped
2 tablespoons parsley,
   chopped
fine dry breadcrumbs

serves 6–8

Place mussels and water in a steamer and steam
mussels open by shaking them over a high flame.
Keep mussels in half shell and arrange on a platter.
   In a saucepan, melt butter, then add salt and
pepper, garlic and parsley. Drizzle butter over mussels.
Sprinkle with breadcrumbs and place under a
preheated hot grill until brown. Serve at once.

* POTATO CROQUETTES *

500 g (1 lb) potatoes, peeled
30 g (1 oz) butter
1 egg yolk
2 tablespoons hot milk
salt and freshly ground black
  pepper, to taste
seasoned flour (see glossary)
2 eggs, beaten
breadcrumbs for coating
olive oil for frying

serves 6

Cook potatoes in boiling, salted water until tender. Drain, then dry potatoes with a tea towel. Mash and press through a sieve or potato ricer. Return to pan. Add butter, egg yolk, milk, and salt and pepper, and beat until smooth. Divide mixture into small pieces similar to the shape of wine corks.

Roll croquettes in seasoned flour, then brush with egg and roll in breadcrumbs. Deep-fry in hot oil until golden brown.

* QUICHE *

Pastry

250 g (8 oz) self-raising (self-rising) flour
185 g (6 oz) hard butter, grated
1 egg yolk
60 ml (¼ cup) cold milk

Filling

625 ml (2½ cups) milk
3 eggs
3 spring onions (scallions), chopped
125 g (4 oz) ham, chopped
125 g (4 oz) cheese, grated

serves 4

Preheat oven to 200°C (400°F).

To make the pastry, sift flour into a large bowl and add butter. Mix with your fingertips until mixture resembles breadcrumbs. Use your fingertips to break up large lumps. Make a hollow in the centre and drop in the egg yolk. Mix again with your fingertips. Pour in milk, a little at a time, until you can make a ball of pastry that sticks together. On a floured surface, roll out the pastry until it is 5 mm (¼ in) thick. Place the pastry in a flan ring or pie dish and trim off the edges. Put it into the refrigerator, covered, for about 30 minutes.

To make the filling, pour milk into a large bowl, break eggs in and beat with an egg beater. Stir onion and ham into the mixture and pour into the pastry shell. Sprinkle cheese over the top and bake in the oven for 45 minutes, or until the quiche is set.

☀ SALMON POTATO CAKES ☀

1 kg (2 lb) boiled potatoes,
  peeled
60 g (2 oz) butter
freshly ground black pepper,
  to taste
2 hard-boiled eggs, chopped
250 g (8 oz) salmon, poached
  and flaked
salt and freshly ground black
  pepper, to taste
1 egg, beaten
fine breadcrumbs, for coating
olive oil, for frying

serves 6

Mash potatoes with butter and pepper and divide into 24 small portions. Shape each portion into a small flat cake, about 5 mm (¼ in) thick.

Mix hard-boiled eggs and salmon in a bowl. Season with salt and pepper.

Place a spoonful of the salmon mixture on a potato cake and cover with another potato cake, pressing edges firmly together to seal. Dip each cake in beaten egg, then coat with breadcrumbs.

Fry in olive oil until golden brown, then drain on absorbent paper and serve immediately.

* SALMON QUICHE *

Pastry

60 g (2 oz) white flour, sifted
60 g (2 oz) wholemeal flour
½ teaspoon salt
90 g (3 oz) butter
1 egg yolk
1 tablespoon lemon juice

Filling

4 slices bacon, rind removed
* and diced*
250 g (8 oz) tin salmon in
* brine*
3 eggs
375 ml (1½ cups) fresh cream
1 tablespoon parsley, chopped
1 tablespoon parmesan
* cheese, grated*
½ teaspoon paprika
1 teaspoon salt
freshly ground black pepper,
* to taste*

serves 6

Preheat oven to 200°C (400°F).

To make pastry, mix flours and salt together in a bowl. Rub in the butter with your fingertips, until the mixture resembles fine breadcrumbs. Add egg yolk and lemon juice and mix to form a firm dough (if necessary, add a tablespoon of water). Press the pastry into a 25 cm (10 in) flan tin.

To make filling, gently fry bacon in a small frying pan. Drain on absorbent paper. Drain and flake salmon, reserving liquid. Arrange the salmon on the base of the pastry, then sprinkle bacon on top.

In a bowl, beat together reserved salmon liquid, eggs, cream, parsley, cheese, paprika, salt and pepper. Pour mixture gently, over the back of a spoon, into the flan tin to cover salmon and bacon.

Bake in the oven for 10 minutes then reduce heat to 165°C (325°F) and cook a further 30–35 minutes, or until the filling is set.

* SATAY CHICKEN TRIANGLES *

3 small chicken fillets, diced
20 sheets filo pastry
butter, melted

Marinade

60 ml (¼ cup) oil
2 tablespoons white wine
  vinegar
1 tablespoon teriyaki sauce
2 teaspoons sesame oil

Peanut sauce

1 tablespoon tomato ketchup
2 teaspoons chilli sauce
½ cup smooth peanut butter
80 ml (⅓ cup) chicken stock
  (see page 380)
2 teaspoons lemon juice

makes 30 triangles

To make marinade, combine all marinade ingredients in a bowl. Add chicken and marinate for 3–4 hours in the refrigerator.

Preheat oven to 220°C (420°F). Heat an electric frypan or wok, add chicken and half the marinade and stir-fry the chicken for 10 minutes or until golden.

Brush one sheet of filo pastry with butter and top with a second sheet of pastry. Cut pastry lengthwise into 3 strips. Spoon a portion of the filling into the corner of one end of a pastry strip. Fold pastry diagonally over filling, from one corner to the opposite side, to form a triangle. Continue to fold pastry, making a triangle every time, until whole strip is used. Brush triangle with butter on both sides and put on a baking tray. Repeat until all filling and all pastry are used. Bake triangles in the oven for 15 minutes, or until pastry is golden brown and flaking.

In a saucepan, combine the ingredients for the peanut sauce and cook for 2 minutes. Allow to cool slightly before serving.

Serve with peanut sauce, for dipping.

* SAUSAGE ROLLS *

1 quantity flaky pastry
500 g (1 lb) sausage meat
beaten egg, for glazing

**makes 24 small sausage
rolls**

Preheat oven to 220°C (420°F). Divide pastry in half. Cut each half into a 7.5 x 30 cm (3 x 12 in) strip.

Form sausage meat into 2 rolls, each 30 cm (12 in) long. Lay a sausage meat roll close to the edge of each pastry strip. Dampen one side of pastry with water, then fold pastry over and press edges together firmly.

Glaze tops of long sausage roll with beaten egg then cut each roll into 12 pieces. Place rolls on a baking tray and bake in the oven for 15 minutes. Reduce oven temperature to moderately hot (200°C/375°F) and bake for a further 10–15 minutes.

* SCRAMBLED EGGS *

8 eggs
salt and freshly ground black
  pepper, to taste
1 tablespoon fresh herbs,
  finely chopped (optional)
60 g (2 oz) butter

serves 4

In a bowl, beat eggs with salt and pepper. Add herbs (if using). A small amount of herbs may be kept for a garnish.

Place 15 g (½ oz) butter in a frying pan and melt over a low heat. Pour in egg mixture and, using a broad wooden spatula, move egg slowly across pan as it thickens. When almost to thickness desired, remove from heat and add remaining butter. Turn onto a hot plate, sprinkle with herbs and serve at once.

Variation: Finely grated cheese can be added with the final butter.

* SEAFOOD FLAN *

Pastry case

500 g (1 lb) plain (all-
  purpose) flour
½ teaspoon salt
pinch of cayenne pepper
pinch of freshly ground black
  pepper
125 g (4 oz) butter
1 egg yolk
2 teaspoons lemon juice
4–6 teaspoons water

Filling

15 g (½ oz) butter
1 small onion, chopped
3 eggs
1 extra egg yolk
125 ml (½ cup) fresh cream
salt and pepper, to taste
1 teaspoon lemon rind, finely
  grated
375 g (12 oz) mixed shellfish
  (prawns/shrimp, rock
  lobster, oysters and scallops)
2–3 tablespoons warm
  brandy

serves 4–6

Preheat oven to 180°C (350°F). To make pastry, sift flour and seasonings into a bowl. Rub butter into flour with fingertips until mixture resembles breadcrumbs. In another bowl, mix egg yolk, lemon juice and water. Add this to flour and mix with a round-bladed knife to form a stiff dough. Cover with plastic film and place in the refrigerator for 30 minutes.

On a floured surface, roll out pastry and line a 23 cm (9 in) flan tin with it. Prick base of flan, line inside with a circle of greased baking paper and sprinkle with dried beans or peas. Blind bake in the middle shelf of the oven for 15–20 minutes. Do not allow to brown. Remove pastry from oven and remove paper and beans.

To make filling, melt butter in a saucepan, add onion and sauté until soft. Do not let onion brown. In a bowl, whisk eggs, egg yolk, cream, seasonings and lemon rind together. Add to sautéed onion and mix. In another saucepan, heat seafood gently in brandy.

Place seafood in flan tin and gently pour over the egg mixture. Cook in the oven for 25–30 minutes, or until filling is set and golden brown. Serve immediately.

* SHRIMP COCKTAIL *

250 g prawns (shrimp),
  cooked and peeled
4 large lettuce leaves, finely
  shredded
slices of lemon, to garnish

Cocktail sauce

3 tablespoons thick
  mayonnaise (see page 364)
1 tablespoon tomato ketchup,
  or thick tomato purée,
  or skinned fresh sieved
  tomatoes
1 tablespoon Worcestershire
  sauce
2 tablespoons full cream
  or evaporated milk (see
  glossary)

Seasoning

pinch of celery salt (see
  glossary) or chopped celery
onion, finely chopped
lemon juice

serves 4

To make the cocktail sauce, mix all the sauce ingredients together in a bowl. Add seasoning and adjust if necessary.

This dish can be arranged in glasses or small flat plates. Place lettuce in cocktail dish and top with prawns or shrimps, cover with sauce, and garnish with lemon slices. Serve as cold as possible.

* SHRIMP TOAST *

10 green tiger prawns
 (shrimp), peeled
½ small garlic clove, crushed
1 teaspoon soy sauce, plus
 extra
1 teaspoon lemon juice
dash of tabasco sauce
60 g (2 oz) sesame seeds, plus
 extra
8 slices white bread, crusts
 removed
oil for deep-frying

makes 16 triangles

Purée the prawns, garlic, soy sauce, lemon juice, tabasco sauce and half the sesame seeds in a blender or food processor.

Spread mixture over one side of each slice of bread, sprinkle with a few sesame seeds, gently press down sesame seeds and cut bread diagonally, into triangles.

Heat oil for deep-frying in a saucepan or deep-fat fryer to 200°C (400°F), or until a cube of bread browns in 30 seconds. Cook the toasts a few at a time for about 3 minutes, until crisp and golden. Drain on absorbent paper and keep warm while cooking the remainder.

Put a small bowl of soy sauce for dipping in the centre of a large plate and arrange the toasts around and serve.

* THE BASIC OMELETTE *

3 large eggs
salt and freshly ground black
   pepper, to taste
1 tablespoon water
15 g (½ oz) butter

serves 1

Place a pan over low heat and warm slowly. Break eggs into a bowl, add salt and pepper, and water. Beat ingredients with a large fork to mix well, but no more. Over-beaten eggs can become watery.

Raise heat under omelette pan, and add butter. When this begins to show a faint brown colour, pour in eggs. Using a fork, and holding the pan with your hand, stir the mixture in the centre a few times, and bring the eggs from the side of the pan towards the middle. This enables any uncooked liquid to run to the sides and cook more easily. As soon as the underside is a light golden brown, and the centre is creamy, lift the edge of the omelette nearest the pan handle, fold the omelette in half and gently roll it towards the edge.

To turn omelette out, hold the omelette pan with your left hand underneath the handle, turn over with a quick flick of the wrist and flip the omelette onto a warmed plate.

If a filling is to be added, make it beforehand and keep it hot, then spread it on half the cooked surface and fold the side of the omelette with no filling over it. In some cases, as with chopped herbs, the filling is cooked with the egg mixture.

Pasta, rice & noodles

COOKING PASTA

To cook pasta, bring 3.5 L (14 cups) salted water to a brisk boil. Add a small amount of pasta at a time. If you are cooking spaghetti, hold it near the end and gently lower the other end into the boiling water; it gradually softens and curves around the pan as it enters the water. Boil pasta briskly, uncovered, stirring occasionally until just tender. The Italians call it 'al dente'—the pasta should be firm when bitten between the teeth. Do not overcook. Drain in a colander, rinse with hot water and stir through a dash of olive oil and salt (optional).

COOKING RICE

To boil rice to serve 4 people, pour 2 cups of rice into a large saucepan of fast-boiling, salted water and boil for 15 minutes. Rice should be just tender. Drain and serve immediately. To steam rice, wash 2 cups of long grain rice and drain well in a colander. Place rice in a saucepan with 3 cups of water and bring to the boil. Lower heat to medium and cook uncovered until water is absorbed. Remove from heat, empty rice into a colander and steam over fast boiling water for 25–30 minutes.

COOKING NOODLES

Use fresh Asian noodles direct from the packet, as they are usually already cooked and require no further preparation. If you do need to cook noodles it is a good idea to rinse them in cold water and drain them after cooking to remove the starch. Cook noodles for 2 minutes in rapidly boiling water or follow the packet instructions.

BROWN RICE WITH CHEESE

30 g (1 oz) butter
2 tablespoons oil
1½ cup shallots, chopped
500 g (1 lb) brown rice,
    washed and drained
1.5 L (6 cups) chicken stock
    (see page 380), heated
1 teaspoon salt
½ teaspoon freshly ground
    black pepper
250 g (8 oz) Swiss cheese,
    sliced, or 180 g (6 oz)
    grated cheese
parsley sprigs, to garnish

serves 6

Heat butter and oil in a large saucepan. Gently fry shallots until soft and golden. Add rice and fry, stirring continuously, for about 8 minutes. Add stock, salt and pepper and stir through. Cover and simmer for 1 hour. Turn into a buttered ovenproof dish.

Cover top of rice with Swiss cheese and place under a hot grill or a hot oven (220°C/420°F) until cheese melts and turns golden.

Garnish with parsley sprigs and serve hot.

* CANNELLONI STUFFED WITH RICOTTA IN TOMATO SAUCE *

12 cannelloni tubes
3 cups ricotta cheese
2 eggs
4 spring onions (scallions),
  finely sliced
60 g (2 oz) parmesan cheese
salt and freshly ground black
  pepper, to taste
pinch of ground nutmeg
4–6 large ripe tomatoes,
  skinned and chopped
3 tablespoons olive oil
60 g (2 oz) butter

serves 4–6

Preheat oven to 180°C (350°F). Cook cannelloni according to packet instructions. Set aside until ready to fill.

In a bowl, mix ricotta cheese, eggs, spring onions and ¼ cup parmesan cheese thoroughly. Season with salt, pepper and nutmeg.

Place tomatoes in a saucepan and cook, uncovered, until they are a thick pulp, stirring occasionally. Remove from heat and stir in oil gradually.

Drain cannelloni and fill with ricotta cheese mixture. Place filled cannelloni side by side in a single layer in a buttered shallow baking dish. Pour tomato sauce around and over the cannelloni, sprinkle with remaining parmesan cheese and dot with butter. Bake in the oven until bubbling, about 20 minutes. Serve at once.

* FETTUCINE ALFREDO *

250 g (8 oz) fettuccine
125 g (4 oz) butter
125 g (4 oz) parmesan
   cheese, grated
¼ teaspoon salt
freshly ground black pepper,
   to taste
250 ml (1 cup) fresh cream
parsley, finely chopped and
   extra parmesan cheese, to
   garnish

serves 6

Cook fettucine for 15 minutes, or until al dente, in a large saucepan of rapidly boiling, salted water.

Meanwhile, melt butter in a large saucepan, then add parmesan cheese, salt, pepper and cream. Cook over a low heat, stirring constantly, until blended.

Drain fettucine. Immediately add to cheese mixture and toss until pasta is well coated. Place in a heated serving dish, sprinkle with parsley and parmesan cheese and serve at once.

* FRIED RICE *

220 g (7½ oz) rice, uncooked
250 ml (1 cup) water, salted
  for boiling
2 eggs
1 teaspoon oil
250 g (½ lb) lean pork,
  chopped and fried quickly
  in oil
250 g (½ lb) prawns
  (shrimp), cooked and
  chopped
5 mushrooms, thinly sliced
4 shallots (scallions), chopped
salt, to taste
4 teaspoons soy sauce

serves 4–6

Wash rice several times in cold water to remove excess starch. Place rice in a saucepan of boiling, salted water and cook for 15 minutes or until grains are just tender—do not overcook. Drain rice and allow to cool completely.

Beat eggs lightly in a bowl, then heat oil in a frying pan and fry as a thin pancake or omelette. Remove from pan and slice into strips. (If you prefer, eggs can be beaten and added to the rice last, instead of frying beforehand.)

Place enough oil in a large pan to cover the base and heat it. When hot, add prepared rice slowly, to avoid clumping, and stir for about 10 minutes or until rice is thoroughly heated through. Stir vigorously, breaking up any lumps.

Add pork, prawns, mushrooms, shallots and salt, then fold in egg pieces (or beaten egg) and soy sauce. Mix well and serve.

* GNOCCHI *

3 medium-sized potatoes,
  washed
125 g (4 oz) plain (all-
  purpose) flour, sifted
1 egg
1½ teaspoons salt
extra flour
Italian Tomato Sauce (see
  page 362) or Bolognaise
  Sauce (see page 353)
parmesan cheese, grated, to
  garnish

serves 4

Boil unpeeled potatoes until tender. Peel while hot and place in a mixing bowl. Mash potatoes straight away, adding sifted flour, a little at a time, while potatoes are still hot. Add egg and salt and beat until smooth.

Turn onto a well-floured board. Knead, working in enough flour to form a smooth, soft, non-sticky dough. Divide dough into several parts. Roll each to pencil thickness. Cut into 2 cm (¾ in) pieces. With the tines of a floured fork, press each piece so that it curls. Place on waxed paper. Sprinkle lightly with flour. Cook immediately, or within 2 hours.

Add gnocchi a little at a time to a large pan of rapidly boiling salted water with a little oil added. Cook for about 5 minutes, or until gnocchi comes to the surface. Drain and keep warm in a heated bowl until all gnocchi is cooked.

Serve in Tomato Sauce or Bolognaise Sauce, sprinkled with parmesan cheese.

* ITALIAN MARINARA *

1kg (2 lb) marinara mix—
  oysters, scallops, prawns
  (shrimp), crayfish (all
  shelled), fish fillet pieces
60 ml (¼ cup) olive oil
2 cloves garlic, sliced
2 x 425 g (1lb 12 oz) tin
  tomatoes, puréed
1½ teaspoons salt
1 teaspoon oregano
1 teaspoon parsley, chopped
¼ teaspoon freshly ground
  black pepper
2 tablespoons red wine
  (optional)
375 g (12 oz) fettucine or
  spaghetti

serves 6–8

Wash and drain the marinara mix. Heat oil in a large frying pan and sauté marinara mix over a medium heat for 5 minutes. Remove from pan and keep warm. Add garlic to the pan and sauté until golden. Stir in tomatoes, salt, oregano, parsley, pepper and wine (if using). Cook rapidly, uncovered, for 15 minutes, or until sauce has thickened. Stir occasionally. If sauce becomes too thick, add ¼–½ cup water. Add marinara mix and reheat gently.

Meanwhile, cook spaghetti in boiling, salted water and drain. Serve immediately with marinara sauce poured on top.

* LASAGNE *

2 tablespoons olive oil
250 g (8 oz) minced beef
250 g (8 oz) minced pork
1 onion, finely chopped
1 glove garlic, finely chopped
1 teaspoon parsley, chopped
250 g (8 oz) tomato paste
470 ml (16 oz) water
½ teaspoon salt
½ teaspoon freshly ground
   black pepper
250 g (8 oz) lasagne sheets
30 g (1 oz) mozzarella
   cheese, sliced thinly
250 g (8 oz) ricotta cheese,
   crumbed
2 tablespoons romano cheese,
   grated

serves 4–6

Heat oil in saucepan, add beef and pork and brown with onion, garlic and parsley. Stir in tomato paste, water, salt and pepper and simmer for 1½ hours.

Preheat oven to 180°C (350°F). Bring a large saucepan of water to the boil, add 1½ teaspoons salt and the lasagne sheets. Boil for 20 minutes, stirring constantly to prevent noodles sticking, until tender. Drain.

In a greased casserole dish about 5 cm (2 in) deep, arrange alternate layers of lasagne sheets, sauce, mozzarella and ricotta cheese. Repeat layers until noodles and sauce and two cheeses are all used, ending with ricotta cheese. Sprinkle with grated romano cheese and bake in the oven for 25–30 minutes.

* MUSHROOM AND ONION RISOTTO *

30 g (1 oz) butter
1 small onion, chopped or sliced
1 rasher bacon, diced
12 button mushrooms, sliced
300 g (10 oz) arborio rice
375 ml (1½ cups) chicken stock, boiling (see page 380)
125 g (4 oz) cheese, grated
salt and freshly ground black pepper, to taste

serves 4

Melt butter in a heavy-based saucepan, and fry onion, bacon and mushrooms, stirring once or twice, for 3–4 minutes. Stir in rice and cook for 1–2 minutes.

Pour in hot stock gradually, stirring constantly until liquid is absorbed. Continue stirring while adding stock until all liquid is absorbed each time. Cook rice for 30 minutes, or until it is tender. Add extra hot water or stock if necessary.

Stir through cheese, and season with salt and pepper. Serve immediately with fresh herbs, accompanied with tossed salad greens.

* SHRIMP RISOTTO *

500 g (1 lb) prawns (shrimp)
4 tablespoons olive oil
2 small onions, finely
  chopped
1 tablespoon green
  peppercorns
250 g (½ lb) arborio rice
180 ml (¾ cup) dry white
  wine
1 medium size onion, grated
squeeze lemon juice
chopped parsley and zest of
  1 lemon, to garnish

serves 4

Shell prawns and make fish stock by boiling shells in about 970 ml (1½ pints) water to which a pinch of salt has been added. Strain and reserve liquid. Chop prawns and set aside.

Place 2 tablespoons oil in a frying pan and lightly brown onions. Add green peppercorns and rice and cook, stirring constantly, until rice is lightly browned. Add wine. When wine has evaporated, add stock, gradually. Stir very lightly and simmer gently, uncovered, until rice is cooked. Add a little hot water or more wine if rice gets too dry.

Meanwhile, heat remaining oil in a saucepan and add grated onion, lemon juice and chopped prawns. Fry lightly until onion is translucent and prawns are cooked—approximately 3 minutes. Stir through rice and serve sprinkled with parsley and lemon zest.

* RAVIOLI *

Filling
2 tablespoons olive oil

375 g (12 oz) minced beef or
  shredded chicken

250 g (8 oz) cooked spinach
  or frozen spinach, thawed

2 eggs, beaten

1 tablespoon parmesan cheese

¾ teaspoon salt

¼ teaspoon freshly ground
  black pepper

500 g (1lb) basic pasta
  dough (see page 345)

1 quantity Italian tomato
  sauce (see page 362)

grated parmesan or romano
  cheese, to garnish

serves 6

To make filling, heat oil in a frying pan. Add meat and cook until browned, then place meat in a bowl. Prepare and cook spinach, draining it well. Finely chop spinach and mix with meat. Add eggs, parmesan cheese, salt and pepper. Mix well. Set aside until ready to use.

Divide pasta dough into quarters. Roll each quarter until it is 3 mm (⅛ in) thick, and a rectangular shape. Cut dough lengthways (using a pastry cutter, if you have one) into strips 12 cm (5 in) wide. Place 2 teaspoons of filling in the centre of one half of the pastry every 8.5 cm (3½ in), then fold over the other half covering the filling. Seal the whole strip by pressing the long edges together with the tines of a fork. Press the two layers of pastry together between the mounds of filling and cut in the middle between mounds with the pastry cutter, again sealing the cut edges with the tines of a fork.

Add ravioli gradually, about a third at a time, to a large saucepan of rapidly boiling, salted water. Cook for 20 minutes or until tender. Remove with a slotted spoon. Drain well.

Serve topped with heated tomato sauce and sprinkled with parmesan cheese.

* SAFFRON RISOTTO *

60 g (2 oz) butter
1 large onion, finely chopped
500 g (1 lb) long grain rice,
   washed and drained
875 ml (3½ cups) chicken
   stock (see page 380)
1 packet powdered saffron
   or a large pinch of saffron
   strands (see glossary)
2 teaspoons salt
10 whole black peppercorns

serves 6–8

Heat butter in a saucepan and gently fry onion for 5 minutes or until golden. Add rice and fry for 2–3 minutes, until all rice grains are coated with butter.

In a saucepan, heat chicken stock. Add hot stock, saffron, salt and peppercorns to the rice. Bring to the boil, then reduce heat, cover tightly and steam for 20 minutes. Remove cover and fluff up rice gently with a fork.

Serve as an accompaniment to fish, poultry or any kind of meat.

* SEAFOOD RISOTTO *

125 ml (½ cup) olive oil
2 cloves garlic, chopped
1 medium onion, chopped
660 g (21 oz) arborio rice
1 bunch shallots (scallions),
  chopped
1 bunch fresh coriander
  (cilantro), chopped
4 pieces butternut pumpkin,
  cooked
1 L (4 cups) fish stock (see
  page 382)
250 ml (1 cup) white wine
1 kg (2 lb) marinara mix
¾ cup parmesan cheese,
  grated
salt and freshly ground black
  pepper, to taste
3 tablespoons sour cream

serves 6

Heat oil in a large saucepan and gently fry onion and garlic. When onion is translucent, add rice. Stir well, until rice is coated with oil. Add shallots and coriander and cook for a few minutes, then add pumpkin.

Add 250 ml (1 cup) stock, stirring constantly until it is absorbed. Add 250 ml (1 cup) wine and continue to stir. Continue to add stock by the cup (and stir regularly), until all stock is absorbed. It will take about 30 minutes to get the rice to an almost cooked stage.

When rice is almost cooked, fold in the marinara mix and cook for a further 5 minutes. Add parmesan. Season with salt and pepper. Cook for another few minutes, until seafood is done, then stir in sour cream.

Serve in bowls, and sprinkle the last of the parmesan on top.

* SPAGHETTI BOLOGNAISE *

1 tablespoon olive oil
250 g (½ lb) minced beef
1 clove garlic, crushed
1 large onion (or 2 small
  onions), finely grated
500 g (1 lb) peeled tomatoes,
  chopped
1 teaspoon oregano or basil
1 teaspoon salt
freshly ground black pepper,
  to taste
1 teaspoon sugar
3 tablespoons tomato paste
250 ml (1 cup) beef stock
  (see page 378)
250 g (½ lb) spaghetti
parmesan cheese, to garnish

serves 4

Heat oil in frying pan, add meat, garlic and onion and brown lightly. Add tomatoes, oregano, salt, pepper and sugar. In a small bowl, blend tomato paste with stock. Add this to mixture in frying pan. Simmer for 30 minutes, uncovered, so that sauce thickens slightly.

When sauce is almost ready, cook spaghetti in boiling salted water until tender (about 20 minutes). Drain spaghetti, and place on a hot serving dish or plate. Pour hot sauce over spaghetti and sprinkle with parmesan cheese. Serve additional cheese in a small bowl.

* SPAGHETTI CARBONARA *

250–375 g (8–12 oz)
 fettucine
2 tablespoons olive oil
3 slices bacon, finely diced
2 eggs
45 g (1½ oz) parmesan
 cheese, grated
250 ml (1 cup) fresh cream
freshly ground black pepper,
 to taste

serves 4

Add fettucine into boiling, salted water and cook for 8 minutes or until al dente.

Just before fettucine is ready, heat oil and fry bacon.

In a bowl, beat in eggs and add cheese.

Drain pasta and return to the hot saucepan. Add cheese mixture, cream, plenty of black pepper and crisp bacon. Mix well. Place the saucepan over a low heat for a minute or so, stirring constantly.

Place in a hot dish and serve immediately.

* SPAGHETTI WITH MEATBALLS *

Tomato sauce

1 x 500 g (1 lb) can whole
  tomatoes
250 ml (1 cup) Italian
  tomato sauce (see page 362)
125 g (4 oz) tomato paste
60 ml (¼ cup) water
60 ml (¼ cup) red wine
  (or water)
2 bay leaves, crushed
2 tablespoons parsley,
  chopped
1 clove garlic, crushed

Meatballs

4 slices white bread
500 g (1 lb) minced chuck or
  round steak
1 tablespoon parmesan
  cheese, grated
1 tablespoon parsley, chopped
1 tablespoon onion, grated
2 teaspoons salt
¼ teaspoon black pepper
¼ teaspoon oregano
1 egg
3 tablespoons olive oil

To make tomato sauce, combine all ingredients in a large saucepan. Simmer until thick, stirring occasionally for about 10 minutes.

To make meatballs, place bread in a small bowl, add enough water to cover, and let stand for 2 minutes. Remove bread and squeeze out excess water. In a larger bowl, combine bread with minced steak, parmesan cheese, parsley, onion, salt, pepper, oregano and egg. Mix lightly until thoroughly combined. Shape into small balls. Heat oil in a frying pan and brown meatballs on all sides.

Add meatballs to sauce and simmer for 15–20 minutes. Meanwhile, cook spaghetti in salted, boiling water (about 20 minutes). Drain spaghetti and place on a hot serving dish or plate. Top with meatballs and sauce and sprinkle with parmesan cheese.

250 g (8 oz) spaghetti or thin
  spaghetti
parmesan cheese, freshly
  grated, to garnish

serves 4–6

* SPAGHETTI SPRINGTIME *

4–6 tomatoes, skinned and
  chopped
250 g (8 oz) cooked hot
  spaghetti, drained
1 green capsicum (bell
  pepper), chopped
½ cup spring onions
  (scallions), chopped
¼ cup black olives, chopped
salt and freshly ground black
  pepper, to taste
juice of half a lemon
80 ml (⅓ cup) olive oil
chopped parsley, to garnish
parmesan cheese (optional)

serves 6–8

Put tomatoes into a saucepan and heat, stirring.
When they are hot, add spaghetti, capsicum, spring
onions, olives, salt and pepper, lemon juice, and
enough olive oil to coat pasta. Toss well.

Sprinkle with parsley and parmesan cheese (if
using) and serve immediately.

* TUNA AND RICE BAKE *

Rice crust
750 ml (3 cups) water
1¼ cups uncooked brown rice, well washed and drained
⅓ cup shallots (scallions), chopped
1 egg, lightly beaten
1 teaspoon curry powder
1½ tablespoons butter, melted

Filling
1 x 425 g (13½ oz) can tuna in brine, drained (reserve liquid)
1 carrot, grated
1 zucchini (courgette), grated
60 g (2 oz) butter
30 g (1 oz) cup flour
1 teaspoon dry mustard (see glossary)
1 teaspoon paprika, plus extra (see glossary), to garnish
½ teaspoon freshly ground black pepper
375 ml (1½ cups) milk
2 tablespoons parsley, chopped
2 teaspoons lemon juice
60 g (2 oz) tasty cheese, grated
thin lemon slices and chopped parsley, to garnish

serves 8

In a large saucepan, bring water to the boil. Slowly add rice. Stir once with a fork, then cover tightly with a lid. Simmer gently until all liquid is absorbed (45–50 minutes).

Preheat oven to 200°C (375°F). In a bowl, combine cooked rice with shallots, egg, curry powder and butter. Press onto base and sides of a 23 cm (9 in) square ovenproof dish.

Spread tuna evenly over rice base. Top with carrot and zucchini and set aside.

Melt butter in a saucepan, then add flour, mustard, paprika and pepper and cook for 1 minute, mixing well. Gradually blend in milk and reserved tuna liquid, and bring mixture to the boil. Then add parsley and lemon juice, and stir until smooth.

Pour sauce over vegetables, and sprinkle over cheese and paprika. Bake in the oven for 30 minutes until heated through. Serve garnished with lemon slices and chopped parsley.

Fish & seafood

COOKING FISH

For maximum freshness and flavour, buy your fresh fish on the day you intend eating it—don't store it in the refrigerator for a long time. If fish isn't prepared on the day, you can freeze it. As a general guide, allow 500 g (1 lb) of fish for each person if it includes the head and bones. When fish is filleted or cut into steaks, allow 125–250 g (4–8 oz) per person, depending on the recipe being prepared and the accompaniments being served.

Most fish shops will fillet the whole fish you buy, but if you prefer to fillet your own, here's an easy way to do it. Make a cut at the back of the head with a sharp, thin-bladed knife. Keeping close to the backbone, cut right down the tail and gently lift the fillet from the backbone using a slicing motion. Remove fins with scissors. Turn fish and repeat the process. Remove excess bones from fillets with knife or tweezers.

Whichever way you plan to cook your fish, there is usually no lengthy cooking time involved. The moment the flesh is white, moist, and flakes easily when tested with a fork, the fish is ready to eat.

GRILLING

One of the easiest ways of cooking fish is grilling—it is also a healthy method of cooking fish. Small whole fish, or steaks and fillets of larger fish and shellfish can all be grilled. Preheat the griller to a moderate heat and place the fish on the grill tray to cook. Alternatively, line a grill pan with aluminium foil and cook your fish on the stove top, regularly basting the fish while cooking (combined melted butter and lemon juice is tasty). Herbs, finely chopped onion, white wine or other seasonings of your choice may also be added to the basting sauce. The fish will be cooked in approximately 10 minutes, depending on its size and thickness. Turn the fish once only while cooking as it breaks easily—constant turning is not necessary.

FRYING

Fish may be shallow or deep fried. Deep-frying is ideal for smaller fillets of fish, or shellfish coated with batter. Shallow frying is used for fish fillets or steaks and small whole fish. Always dry pieces of fish well with absorbent paper before cooking. Most fish is coated before frying to protect the delicate flesh and keep it moist. Seasoned flour and egg and breadcrumbs are two ways of coating fish. Use peanut or avocado oil for deep-frying. For shallow frying, olive oil or butter or a combination of the two may be used.

Make sure the oil is very hot before adding prepared fish. Cook the fish quickly and when golden brown on both sides, remove the fish with a metal spatula or slotted spoon and drain on absorbent paper. Serve immediately while the fish is moist inside and the coating is crisp.

COATINGS FOR FRIED FISH

1 Plain (all-purpose) flour seasoned with pepper. (Salt is best added after the fish is fried.) Dry fish well and coat lightly with flour, shaking off any surplus. Small fish may be coated easily by shaking them gently in a plastic bag containing a little flour.

2 Egg and breadcrumbs. A deliciously crisp coating for fish. Dip pieces of fish in slightly beaten egg which has been diluted with a spoonful of water or oil. Coat with fine dry breadcrumbs (or crushed breakfast cereal for a different flavour) pressing the crumbs on firmly. Stand fish for at least 15 minutes before frying (the crumbs will then stay on when frying).

3 Add freshly ground black pepper, paprika, finely chopped herbs, grated parmesan cheese or other seasonings to crumbs before coating fish, but again it is best to add salt after frying.

4 Batter is a delicious way of coating fish providing the mixture is thin and light and the cooked fish is eaten immediately while moist inside and the batter is golden brown and crisp (batter recipe see page 344).

POACHING

This is cooking fish in a gentle simmering liquid. This method is ideal for whole fish like salmon and trout, or smoked fish. A fish kettle is ideal for poaching fish. It has an inner perforated tray to place the fish on, and when cooked, the tray can be lifted out without breaking the fish. If a fish kettle is not available, poach fish in an ordinary saucepan, but wrap it in a piece of muslin first so that it will not break up while cooking and it can be lifted out of the liquid easily. Salt water, fish stock or milk may be used as a poaching liquid. The fish should be completely covered with liquid while cooking.

    Bring the liquid to the boil and immerse the fish. Return the liquid to the boil, then immediately lower the heat until the liquid is just simmering gently. Allow 6–10 minutes per 500g (1lb) of flesh. Remove fish from the pan immediately when the fish is cooked—overcooking means soft fish with little texture or flavour.

STEAMING

An ideal method of cooking delicately flavoured fish or for those wanting an easily digestible food. Fish may be steamed in the upper half of a double boiler (the upper section having a perforated base), over gently simmering water. The fish may be wrapped in aluminium foil to protect the flesh and keep it moist.

    Fillets of fish may also be steamed on a greased plate over a saucepan of gently simmering water. Season with pepper and dot with butter if desired. Cover with a second plate. Cooking should take approximately 10 minutes, depending on size of fillets.

BAKING

Fish may be baked in the oven either whole or filleted. Most fish are best baked whole, as the outer skin protects the flesh and keeps it moist. There are many delicious stuffings for whole fish baked in the oven. Bake in a hot oven 200–230°C (400–450°F). The length of time will depend on the size of the fish. Either bake in a baking dish and baste with butter and lemon juice while cooking or wrap in aluminium foil, placing small pieces of butter over the fish and a little lemon juice or white wine. Fish is cooked when flesh flakes easily with a fork (test the thickest part of the fish).

Small fillets can be baked in a very hot oven 230–260°C (450–550°F). They may be coated with seasoned breadcrumbs, grated cheese, and sliced tomatoes. But if preferred, dot with butter, add a little lemon juice and baste regularly while cooking. The fish will take approximately 10 minutes to cook. The liquid that drains away from the fish while baking should be used in any sauce being made to serve with the fish.

BARBECUING

Whole fish, fish steaks, fillets of fish and shellfish can all be barbecued. Whole fish may be barbecued in wire frames, turning frequently. No basting is required, but when cooked and ready to serve, brush the fish with butter and lemon juice and season with salt and pepper. Small fish, freshly caught, may be threaded on stainless steel skewers for barbecuing or they may be cooked in wire frames placed flat over the fire.

Fish steaks, fillets of fish and shellfish may be barbecued directly over glowing coals or cooked in a cast iron skillet or on a hotplate.

* BAKED FISH *

*1 large snapper, mullet or
  redfish, cleaned*
1 teaspoon salt
¼ teaspoon white pepper
2 onions, sliced
*4 ripe tomatoes, skinned and
  thickly sliced*
*½ teaspoon ground allspice
  (see glossary)*
¼ teaspoon extra salt
*¼ teaspoon black
  peppercorns, crushed*
½ teaspoon cayenne pepper
2 tablespoons brown sugar
125 ml (½ cup) vinegar
60 ml (¼ cup) water
60 g (2 oz) butter

serves 4–6

Preheat oven to 150°C (300°F). Place fish in a greased baking dish and season with salt and pepper. Cover with onion and tomato. Sprinkle with allspice, extra salt, peppercorns, cayenne pepper and brown sugar. Add vinegar and water and dot with small pieces of butter.

Bake fish in the oven for 20–30 minutes, depending on the size of fish. Baste frequently. Serve with a green salad or vegetable.

* CRAYFISH MORNAY *

1 x 1 kg (2 lb) crayfish
1 shallot, finely chopped
salt and freshly ground black
  pepper, to taste
cayenne pepper, to taste
paprika, to taste
30 g (1 oz) butter
150 ml (⅔ cup) mornay
  sauce, heated (see page
  191)
parsley sprigs, to garnish

serves 2

Wash crayfish well under warm water, then remove its head and cut the shell in half, removing the intestines at the same time. Scoop meat from shell and cut into 2 cm (1 in) cubes. Place shell halves in a hot oven (220°C/420°F) until bright red in colour.

Place crayfish meat into a bowl, and add shallot, salt and pepper, and a dash of cayenne pepper. Place mixture in hot shells, sprinkle with paprika, dot with butter and place under a hot grill until the meat becomes clear white and loses its transparent appearance. Coat with mornay sauce, and replace under hot grill briefly, until golden brown—overcooking will toughen the crayfish.

Serve garnished with parsley sprigs and accompanied by thinly sliced fried potatoes and sautéed mushrooms.

* DEEP-FRIED FISH *

Use fillets of fish and cover with a suitable coating before frying.

For coating, use one of the following:
seasoned flour, for sardines and anchovies
milk and seasoned flour, for fish fillets
seasoned flour, beaten egg and breadcrumbs, for prawns (shrimp)
batter (see page 344), for fish fillets

To make seasoned flour, add a pinch of salt and pepper to plain (all-purpose) flour. You can also add mixed herbs for a more intense flavour.

To deep-fry fish, heat enough oil to cover fish in a deep-frying pan or electric fryer. Test temperature by putting in a 2.5 cm (1 in) cube of bread—it should brown in 1 minute when the oil is at the correct temperature. Place coated fish in oil, avoiding contact between pieces. Cook for 2–3 minutes. Drain well on absorbent paper.

Serve piping hot with lemon wedges, potato chips and tartare sauce (see page 372).

* SNAPPER FILLETS WITH WHITE WINE AND PARSLEY *

½ cup plain flour
1 teaspoon coarse ground
  pepper
¼ teaspoon sea salt
4 snapper fillets, about 220 g
  (8 oz) each
2 tablespoons olive oil
60 g (2 oz) butter
2 cloves garlic, crushed
½ cup white wine
¼ cup parsley, finely chopped

serves 4

Combine the flour, pepper and salt in a dish and coat the fish fillets evenly, shaking off any excess.

Heat the oil in a pan, add the fish, and cook over a medium heat for 5–6 minutes on each side, depending on thickness of fish. Set fish aside on a plate, and keep warm.

Wipe out the pan, then melt butter, add garlic, and cook for 2 minutes. Add the white wine and simmer until the sauce reduces.

Just before serving, add chopped parsley to the sauce and serve with the fish.

* FRIED LOBSTER WITH BUTTER *

1 medium-sized rock lobster
½ teaspoon salt
1 teaspoon plain flour
olive oil, for frying
juice from half a lemon
lemon wedges and finely
  chopped parsley, to garnish

serves 2

Cut lobster in half lengthways, then remove the bag in the head and intestine.

Sprinkle lobster meat with salt and flour. Heat olive oil in a pan and add lobster, cut side down. Fry for 15 minutes, then turn and fry for another 15 minutes. Place lobster on plate and squeeze over lemon juice.

Garnish with lemon wedges and serve with tossed salad greens.

* FRIED WHITEBAIT *

500 g (1 lb) fresh whitebait
plain (all-purpose) flour, for
   coating
olive oil for frying
rock salt, crushed
sliced lemon and fresh bread
   and butter, for serving

serves 4

Rinse whitebait and drain well, then dry with absorbent paper. Toss lightly in flour and place in a wire basket. Fry in deep, hot oil. Drain well.

Reheat oil and fry whitebait again, until very crisp. Drain on absorbent paper again, then sprinkle with rock salt and serve with lemon and bread and butter.

* FRIED WHITING *

2–3 tablespoons lemon juice
1 onion, sliced
1 bouquet garni (see glossary)
500 g (1 lb) fresh whiting
   fillets
3 egg yolks, beaten
1 teaspoon water
3 tablespoons parmesan
   cheese, finely grated
butter, for frying
lemon wedges, for serving

serves 4–6

Combine lemon juice, onion and bouquet garni and pour over fish. Let fish and liquid stand for 1 hour; turn fish once or twice during the hour.

In a bowl, whisk together egg yolks and water. Put parmesan cheese into another bowl, or onto a flat board, or into a clean plastic bag. Dip each piece of fish in the egg mixture, then cover it with grated cheese.

Heat butter and fry fish for approximately 20 minutes, turning once while cooking, or until cooked through and golden brown.

Serve with potato wedges and a salad.

* LOBSTER THERMIDOR *

90 g (3 oz) butter
30 g (1 oz) plain (all-
  purpose) flour
270 ml (⅜ pint) milk
2 tablespoons thickened
  cream
Dijon mustard
salt and black pepper, to taste
2 medium-sized lobsters,
  meat removed from shells
  and diced
1 small onion or eschalot,
  finely chopped
2 tablespoons white wine or
  sherry
60 g (2 oz) parmesan cheese,
  grated

serves 4

In a saucepan, melt 30 g (1 oz) butter. Add the flour, mix well and cook for 1–2 minutes. Stir in milk, cream, a little mustard and salt and pepper. Add the lobster meat and heat gently.

In another pan, melt the remaining butter and fry the onion or shallot. Add to lobster mixture, together with wine. Pile mixture into lobster shells, cover tops with grated parmesan cheese and brown under a hot grill.

* OYSTERS MORNAY *

12 large, flat oysters
salt and pepper, to taste
1 tablespoon parmesan
  cheese, grated

Mornay sauce
15 g (½ oz) butter
1 tablespoon plain (all-
  purpose) flour
150 ml (⅔ cup) milk
60 g (2 oz) gruyère cheese,
  grated
salt and freshly ground black
  pepper, to taste
1–2 tablespoons fresh cream

serves 1–2

Sprinkle oysters with salt and pepper and place under a hot grill for 1 minute. Spread each oyster with mornay sauce to cover. Sprinkle with parmesan cheese and bake in a hot oven for 5–10 minutes or until golden brown. Serve immediately.

To make Mornay Sauce, melt butter in a small saucepan. Blend in flour until smooth, then cook for 1–2 minutes. Add milk and bring to the boil, stirring continuously. Remove pan from heat and add cheese. Stir until cheese melts. Season with salt and pepper and add enough cream to make the sauce a good coating consistency.

* OYSTERS MICHELENE *

12 oysters
120 g (4 oz) prawns
 (shrimp), peeled and
 deveined
30 g (1 oz) butter
cayenne pepper, to taste

serves 1–2

Preheat oven to 220°C (420°F). Remove oysters from shells and set shells aside. Mix oysters with prawns and chop finely. Mix with butter and cayenne pepper. Place mixture in oyster shells and cook in the oven for 3 minutes. Serve immediately.

* OYSTERS NATURAL *

12 oysters
lemon wedges

Cocktail sauce
2 tablespoons tomato ketchup
1 teaspoon Worcestershire
 sauce
2 teaspoons cream
pinch of ground black pepper

serves 1–2

Arrange oysters on a bed of crushed ice with lemon wedges. Serve with chilled cocktail sauce in a small bowl in the centre of the plate.

To make Cocktail Sauce, combine all ingredients together until well blended.

✻ POACHED FISH IN WHITE WINE SAUCE ✻

750 g–1 kg (1½–2 lb) fish
  fillets (bream or sole)
375 ml (1½ cups) court
  bouillon (see page 380)
375 ml (1½ cups) dry white
  wine
pinch of tarragon
1 small onion, finely chopped
3 egg yolks
3 tablespoons fresh cream
salt and pepper, to taste

serves 4

Prepare fish and poach in court bouillon. Drain well and keep hot. Place wine, tarragon and onion in a saucepan and bring to the boil. Add court bouillon and boil continuously, until volume is reduced by half. Allow to cool.

In a bowl, beat egg yolks with cream. Add to cooled liquid and reheat gently, without boiling. Season with salt and pepper, pour over the poached fish fillets, and serve.

* SEAFOOD CHOWDER *

500 g (1 lb) marinara mix—
  fish pieces, shelled prawns
  (shrimp), oysters, scallops,
  crab
750 ml (3 cups) water
30 g (1 oz) butter
1 onion, sliced
1 potato, sliced
½ teaspoon saffron
  (optional—see glossary)
salt, to taste
250 ml (1 cup) milk
60–125 ml (¼–½ cup) fresh
  cream
salt and freshly ground black
  pepper, to taste
1 tablespoon parsley, finely
  chopped to garnish

serves 4–6

Poach seafood in salted water until just tender. Strain stock, taking care to remove any skin or bones from fish and set aside. Reserve seafood for later.

Melt butter in a saucepan and sauté onion and potato for 2 minutes. Add strained stock, saffron and salt. Simmer for 20 minutes, then purée in a blender or food processor until smooth.

Return soup to saucepan, add milk and bring to the boil. Add cream and seafood and season to taste. Heat gently but do not boil.

Sprinkle with parsley and serve with crusty bread.

* SEAFOOD PAELLA *

60 ml (¼ cup) olive oil
2 tablespoons butter
2 cloves garlic, chopped
1 onion, chopped
1 capsicum (bell pepper),
  seeded and chopped
3 tomatoes, peeled
330 g (10½ oz) short grain
  rice
825 ml (3¼ cups) fish stock
  (see page 382)
1 teaspoon salt
¼ teaspoon saffron threads,
  crumbled (see glossary)
mixture of seafood—prawns
  (shrimp) (peeled and
  deveined), scallops, mussels,
  uncooked crab
¼ teaspoon freshly ground
  black pepper
3 tablespoons fresh parsley,
  chopped
2 teaspoons fresh oregano,
  chopped
1 teaspoon fresh thyme,
  chopped

serves 8

In a large frying pan (that has a lid), heat oil and butter over a medium heat. Add garlic, onion and capsicum, and cook until tender (about 10 minutes). Stir in tomatoes and cook for about 5 minutes. Add rice and stir. Then stir in fish stock, salt and saffron. Cover and bring to boil, then remove lid, reduce heat and simmer for 5 minutes, stirring continually. Add seafood, then cover and simmer for a further 5 minutes. Add pepper, parsley, oregano, thyme and cook, still covered, until tender (about 10–15 minutes).

* SWEET AND SOUR TUNA *

2 small green capsicums (bell
    peppers), pith and seeds
    removed and cut into thin
    strips
470 g (15 oz) can pineapple
    pieces and 250 ml (1 cup)
    syrup from can
60 g (2 oz) caster (superfine)
    sugar
1 tablespoon cornflour
30 g (1 oz) butter
1 tablespoon vinegar
2 teaspoons soy sauce
1 x 470 g (15 oz) can tuna
    in water
salt, to taste
220 g (7½ oz) rice, cooked

serves 6

Place capsicum in a saucepan, cover with water and bring to the boil. Drain and set aside.

Drain pineapple and measure syrup (make up to 250 ml/1 cup with water if needed).

In a saucepan, add sugar, cornflour and butter and combine over a medium heat. Gradually add pineapple syrup, vinegar and soy sauce. Bring to the boil, and stir constantly until mixture thickens. Add tuna, salt and rice. Simmer for about 15 minutes and serve.

* TUNA MORNAY *

500 g (1 lb) potatoes, boiled
30 g (1 oz) margarine
2 tablespoons milk
salt and pepper, to taste
300 g (10½ oz) can tuna in
  brine
315 ml (1¼ cups) béchamel
  sauce (see page 351)
30–60 g (2–3 oz) tasty
  cheese, grated

serves 4

Preheat oven to 180°C (350°F). Mash the potatoes and beat in the margarine, milk and salt and pepper. Line the sides and bottom of a shallow ovenproof dish with mashed potato, then put flaked tuna on top of potato on the bottom of the dish. Make (or heat, if it's already made) béchamel sauce, stir in cheese, then spoon sauce over tuna.

Bake in a moderate oven for 15 minutes or until fish is golden on top.

Poultry

* CHICKEN KIEV MACADAMIA *

6 large single chicken breasts,
   boned
salt and freshly ground black
   pepper, to taste
180 g (6 oz) chilled butter,
   cut into 6 even chunks
3 cloves garlic, halved then
   crushed
3 teaspoons parsley, chopped
125 g (4 oz) plain (all-
   purpose) flour, seasoned
   with salt and black pepper
2 eggs, beaten
¼ cup ground macadamia
   nuts
oil, for frying

serves 6

Pound chicken breasts flat with a meat tenderiser.
Sprinkle breasts on both sides with salt and pepper
and lay them skin side down. In the centre of each
breast put 1 chunk of chilled butter, ½ clove crushed
garlic and ½ teaspoon chopped parsley. Roll each
breast in towards the centre, then tie each one
securely with string.

Roll breasts in seasoned flour, dip in egg and then
roll in ground macadamia nuts. Press nuts on firmly
and chill breasts for at least 30 minutes.

Deep-fry breasts in hot oil (190°C/375°F) for 5
minutes. Lift them out and gently remove the string.
Return breasts to oil for 10–12 minutes, or until
cooked. Drain breasts on absorbent paper and serve
immediately.

* CHICKEN SUPREME *

1 x 1.5 kg (3 lb) chicken, cooked and boned
1 large green capsicum (bell pepper), seeds and pith removed and sliced
60 g (2 oz) button mushrooms, washed and cut into quarters
45 g (1½ oz) butter
2 tablespoons plain (all-purpose) flour
315 ml (1¼ cups) chicken stock (see page 380)
3 tablespoons fresh cream
½ teaspoon salt
freshly ground black pepper, to taste

serves 4

Preheat oven to 180°C (350°F). Cut chicken meat into bite-sized pieces.

Blanch capsicum in boiling salted water for 2–3 minutes, then drain. Melt 15 g (½ oz) butter in a frying pan and sauté capsicum and mushrooms for 2–3 minutes. Set aside.

Melt remaining butter in a flameproof casserole dish (use one that has a lid). Add flour and blend until smooth, then cook for 10 minutes until golden. Add stock and bring to the boil, stirring continuously. Add cream and boil rapidly until sauce has a syrupy consistency. Add seasonings, chicken, capsicum and mushrooms. Mix thoroughly, then cover and cook in the oven for 20 minutes, or until hot.

Served on a bed of steamed rice.

* CHICKEN TERIYAKI *

2 tablespoons butter
80 ml (⅓ cup) teriyaki sauce
  or soy sauce
2.5 cm (1 in) piece ginger,
  chopped
2 tablespoons sugar
2 tablespoons dry sherry
500 g (1 lb) (2 large)
  boneless chicken breasts,
  skinned
8 shallots (scallions), cut into
  2.5 cm (1 in) strips
bamboo skewers, soaked in
  water

serves 4

Place butter, teriyaki sauce, ginger, sugar and dry sherry in a small pan and stir over a medium heat until sugar is dissolved. Cool.

Cut chicken into 2.5 cm (1 in) pieces and stir into marinade with shallots. Chill for at least 2 hours.

Thread chicken and shallots onto bamboo skewers and grill for 4–5 minutes on either side, or until cooked, brushing occasionally with marinade.

Serve with steamed rice and salad.

* CURRIED CHICKEN *

1 x 1.5 kg (3 lb) chicken, cut into chunks
60 g (2 oz) butter
2 onions, chopped
1 tablespoon curry powder
1 teaspoon curry paste
1 tablespoon plain (all-purpose) flour
500 ml (2 cups) chicken stock (see page 380)
1 clove garlic, crushed
salt and freshly ground black pepper, to taste
1 tablespoon redcurrant jelly
125 ml (½ cup) coconut milk
60 ml (¼ cup) fresh cream

serves 6

Preheat oven to 180°C (350°F). Melt butter in a flameproof casserole dish (use one that has a lid) and fry chicken until golden brown. Remove chicken and sauté onion in remaining butter until golden. Add curry powder and paste and continue to cook for 3–4 minutes. Add flour and blend until smooth. Stirring continuously, add stock and bring to the boil. Replace chicken in casserole, add garlic and season with salt and pepper.

Cover casserole dish and cook in the oven for 45 minutes, or until chicken is tender. Place chicken on a serving dish and keep warm. Add redcurrant jelly and coconut milk to curry sauce, bring to the boil and simmer for 5 minutes. Add cream and spoon sauce over chicken pieces.

Serve with boiled rice and chutney.

* EASY CURRIED CHICKEN *

60 g (2 oz) butter
1 kg (2 lb) chicken breast,
   sliced into 2 cm strips
2 teaspoons curry powder
1 onion, diced
2 rashers bacon, diced
2 carrots, sliced
1 stick celery, sliced
1 cup peas, cooked
470 g (15 oz) can tomatoes
1 tablespoon pickles, diced
1 teaspoon tomato sauce
1 teaspoon Worcestershire
   sauce

serves 6

Melt half the butter in a frying pan and quickly fry the chicken strips. The chicken should be coloured on the outside, and still pink in the middle. Set aside.

Melt remaining butter in a frying pan and add curry powder (use more than suggested if you like your curries hot). Add onion and bacon and fry for 5 minutes ot until soft. Add remaining ingredients. If the dish seems to be too dry, add 180 ml (¾ cup) water with 2 beef stock cubes dissolved in it. Lastly add the chicken and simmer for 1 hour.

Serve with boiled or steamed rice and condiments such as desiccated coconut, cucumber sliced into yoghurt and fruit chutney.

* GARLIC AND HERB CHICKEN *

90 g (3 oz) butter, softened
1 garlic clove, crushed
2 tablespoons shallots
    (scallions), chopped
2 tablespoons parsley,
    chopped
2 teaspoons prepared mustard
4 chicken maryland pieces
    (see glossary)
pinch of paprika
baking paper
aluminium foil

serves 4

Preheat oven to 200°C (400°F).

In a bowl, combine butter with garlic, shallots, parsley and mustard, and mix well. Carefully lift skin from flesh of chicken, and spread flavoured butter over flesh. Dust chicken pieces with paprika, then wrap chicken individually in baking paper, and then in foil.

Bake in the oven for 20 minutes, then open foil and baking paper and cook for a further 20 minutes.

Serve with tossed salad.

* ROAST CHICKEN *

1 x 1.5 kg (3 lb) chicken,
  washed and dried
salt and freshly ground black
  pepper, to taste
3 tablespoons olive oil
315 ml (½ pint) chicken
  stock (see page 380)

serves 6

Preheat oven to 180°C (350°F). Rub chicken with salt, pepper and half the olive oil. Truss chicken and place in a greased roasting pan with remaining oil. Cook in the oven, basting occasionally, for 1 hour, or until tender and golden brown all over. Remove chicken and keep warm. While chicken is cooking make chicken stock.

Add chicken stock to pan juices and bring to the boil. Strain into a sauceboat and serve with chicken, roast potatoes and green vegetables.

* SAUTÉED CHICKEN *

1 x 2 kg (4 lb) chicken
flour, to coat
90 g (3 oz) butter
salt and freshly ground black
  pepper, to taste
250 ml (1 cup) dry white
  wine
chopped parsley or chives, to
  garnish

serves 4

Cut chicken into 4 joints and dip in flour. Heat butter in a large, heavy, deep-frying pan and brown chicken pieces, turning each piece so that it colours evenly. When browned, add salt and pepper and wine. Reduce heat, cover and continue cooking for 30 minutes or until chicken is tender. Turn chicken pieces two or three times during cooking to absorb the flavours.

When chicken is cooked, remove and keep warm. Add a little more wine if the pan is quite dry, and let pan juices cook over increased heat for a few minutes.

Pour sauce over chicken, garnish with chopped parsley or chives and serve.

* SOUTHERN FRIED CHICKEN *

1 chicken
60 g (2 oz) flour
salt and freshly ground black
 pepper, to taste
1 teaspoon paprika
 (optional)
125 g (4 oz) butter or olive
 oil, for frying
gravy, to serve (see page 357)
grilled pineapple, to serve
grilled tomatoes, to serve

serves 4–6

Disjoint the chicken and soak it in salted water for 10 minutes. Shake off excess water.

In a large paper bag, shake flour, salt and pepper and paprika (if using) together to mix. Put chicken pieces in the bag and shake thoroughly to coat.

In a large frying pan, heat butter and fry all chicken pieces together over a high heat until golden brown on one side. Turn pieces over, lower heat and continue to fry, turning occasionally, until meat is tender (30–40 minutes, depending on size of chicken).

Drain and serve hot with gravy and grilled pineapple and tomatoes.

* CHICKEN DRUMETTES *

¼ cup olive oil
¼ cup tomato sauce
2 tablespoons honey
1 tablespoon barbecue sauce
1 tablespoon Dijon mustard
3 teaspoons Worcestershire
  sauce
2 cloves garlic, crushed
1 kg (36 oz) chicken
  drumettes
parsley, to garnish

makes 18-20

Combine olive oil, tomato sauce, honey, barbecue sauce, Dijon mustard, Worcestershire sauce and garlic in a shallow dish.

Add chicken and coat well in mixture. Cover with plastic wrap and place in the refrigerator to marinate for 2–3 hours.

Preheat the oven to 200°C (400°F). Line a baking tray with foil. Place chicken on a rack over the baking tray. Bake in the oven for 30–35 minutes or until cooked. Garnish with parsley, to serve.

Meat

POT ROASTING

This is one of the simplest ways of cooking a joint of meat. It is a slow method of cooking which makes tough meat moist, tender and tasty. It is important to have the right type of pot or casserole dish. It should be of thick iron, enamelled cast iron, aluminium or flameproof pottery, and big enough to hold a joint comfortably and with a close-fitting lid.

First, the meat is browned all over in the pot, using 1–2 tablespoons of olive oil. Then add an onion stuck with 2–3 cloves, a bouquet garni and salt and pepper. Don't add liquid unless the recipe tells you to; it will usually not be more than 75 ml (⅓ cup) stock or wine. You can also add a thick layer of vegetables—whole potatoes, carrots, turnips, onions—into the pan. Cut the vegetables into pieces so that they will be well done but not overcooked when the meat is done.

Put the lid on and place the pot over a very low heat or into a slow oven (150°C/300°F), allowing approximately 30 minutes per 500 g (1 lb).

BEEF
Allow about 25–30 minutes per 500 g (1 lb) and 25–30 minutes over, depending upon how well done you like it.

CHICKEN
Allow 20–25 minutes per 500 g (1 lb) and 20–25 minutes over. Remember to weigh the chicken after you have stuffed it (see page 290 for stuffing recipe).

LAMB, MUTTON, VEAL
Allow 35–40 minutes per 500 g (1 lb) and 35–40 minutes over.

GRILLING

Grilling requires a certain amount of attention. Heat the grill first until it is red hot. While it is heating, also heat the grill rack in the grill pan underneath. If raw meat is placed on a hot grill rack it will not stick to it during cooking.

Brush the meat lightly with olive oil. Do not salt it; this causes the juices to run out, and you will lose some of the natural flavour and nutritional value of the meat. Place the prepared meat under the red-hot grill and cook until it changes colour from red-pink to brown (1–2 minutes). This means the surface of the meat has seared and the juices are sealed in. Turn the meat over and sear the other side, then continue to grill for the required cooking time, or until the meat is cooked to your taste. Turn the meat with tongs or two spoons to avoid piercing the seal. If you need to slow the cooking down, move the grill pan down, further away from the red hot grill, rather than reducing the temperature of the grill.

Cooking times for grilling meat depend on the cut, the thickness and your own taste. When a cooked steak is pressed with your fingers it feels like a sponge if it's rare, is firmer and less spongy if it's medium, and is quite firm, with no give, when well done. Grilled steaks should be served immediately.

Cuts	Degree	Grilling Times in minutes
rump steak 750 g (2.5 cm/1 in thick) serves 3–4	rare medium rare well done	6–7 8–10 14–16
sirloin or rib steak 2–2.5 cm (¾–1 in thick) serves 1well done	rare medium rare 9–10	5 6–7
minute steak (thin slice of rib steak) 1 cm (½ in) thick, serves 1	rare medium rare	1 2–3
t-bone steak 3.5–5 cm (1½–2 in) thick serves 2–3	rare medium rare	7–8 8–10
porterhouse steak 3.5–5 cm (1½–2 in) thick serves 1–2	rare medium rare	7–8 8–10
fillet steak 2.5–3.5 cm (1–1½ in thick) serves 1well done	rare medium rare to 7–8	6

Cuts	Degree	Grilling Times in minutes
tournedos 2.5–3.5 cm (1–1½ in) thick serves 1	rare medium rare to well done	6 7–8
chateaubriand 8–10 cm (3¼–4 in) thick serves 2	rare to medium rare	16–20
pork chops	well done	15–20
lamb chops		8–10
sausages	thick thin	10–15 8–10
kidneys	10	
bacon	rasher	3–4

FRYING

Frying is a quick method of cooking. There are two methods of frying: deep and shallow. Meat is seldom deep fried. Steak, chops, cutlets and veal cordon bleu are often shallow fried. Meat is often shallow fried as a first stage—this is done when you are making stews, braising or pot roasting.

When frying meat, choose the fat or oil which most complements the natural flavour of the meat: butter is best for juicy fillet steak and delicate wiener schnitzel; a mixture of butter and oil is ideal for most meats, and the oil stops the butter burning; olive oil gives an authentic flavour to Mediterranean meat dishes; and peanut oil is used for Oriental meat dishes, such as stir-fries.

Frying is not always done in a frying pan in meat cookery; it's often done in a saucepan or a flameproof casserole. Whatever is used, make sure it has a heavy base which will distribute the heat evenly. This will help ensure that the meat doesn't burn or stick.

When you are shallow frying meat in a frying pan, the fat should cover the base of the pan, and in some recipes it should come halfway up the meat, so that the sides are completely cooked (with crumbed cutlets, for example). Turn the food once only and remember that the surface of the food which is fried first is the most attractive, and so should be served uppermost.

If the piece of meat you are cooking is thick (more than 2.5 cm/1 in thick), cook it on a moderate heat after first browning it on a high heat. The brown sediment left in the pan after frying meat is the concentrated meat juices. To make a quick gravy from this, first pour off the excess fat. Then reheat the frying pan adding a little water, stock or wine. When the liquid has reduced to a gravy consistency, pour it over the meat.

STEWING

Stewing is cooking food slowly and gently in liquid. Meat can be stewed either on top of the stove or in the oven. During stewing, the liquid should simmer gently, with bubbles just breaking the surface. Meat for stewing is usually from less tender cuts. It will have a slight marbling of fat or gristle, and requires long, slow cooking. During the stewing the gristle is changed into gelatine, which means the meat becomes tender; the fat gives flavour to the stew. If you allow the liquid to boil rapidly, the meat will become tough.

Meat stews can be either brown or white. In a brown stew the meat is browned in fat first, and some flour is often added and browned to give extra colour and flavour. Vegetables may also be browned to add to the colour and flavour. Enough stock is added to come to just below the top of the meat. The pan or casserole is then covered, and the stew is cooked slowly on top of the stove or in the oven, until the meat is tender. A flameproof casserole is ideal for cooking stews, but you can do the preliminary frying in a frying pan or large saucepan and then transfer the meat to an ovenproof casserole. Stews are usually served direct from the casserole.

In a white stew (often called a fricassee), the meat is not browned. Instead, it is often blanched first to whiten it and remove strong flavours. A white stew is cooked on top of the stove and is thickened after the meat is cooked.

BOILING

Boiling is cooking food covered with water at boiling point. In the case of boiling meat, put the joint into boiling, salted water and bring it back to the boil to seal the outside and seal in the meat juices. Then reduce the heat and cook the meat in simmering water until tender. Allow 20–25 minutes per 500g (1 lb) and 20–25 minutes over.

SAUTÉING

Meat used for sautéing must be young, tender and of best quality, such as pork and veal fillet. Sautéing is frying meat lightly in a small quantity of butter and/or oil to seal in the juices. A small quantity of stock or wine is added during the cooking process to come level with the top of the meat, and this is simmered a little to reduce the sauce and concentrate the flavour. The sauce can be thickened at this point if you prefer it thicker.

If you want to create a sauce for your meat whilst cooking it, a sauté pan should be used. A sauté pan is a 7 cm (2½ in) deep , straight-sided, heavy frying pan with a lid. The wide base allows room for browning, and for quick reduction of the sauce. The lid is used if you need to slow down reduction of the sauce, and ensures complete cooking of the meat because it keeps the moisture and heat in the pan. A deep-frying pan with a lid can also be used.

BRAISING

Braising is an ideal method of cooking cheaper, tougher cuts of meat. Braising is a combination of steaming and baking: the meat is cooked in a heavy pot on top of a bed of vegetables, with liquid coming a quarter of the way up the side of the meat. Braising can be done on top of the stove or in the oven in a heavy flameproof cast-iron casserole dish. A whole joint can be braised, or meat can be cut into 5 cm (2 in) cubes and braised, in the case of ragouts.

First, brown the meat in fat in the pot. Put it aside. Then sauté a mixture of root vegetables, cut into chunky pieces, gently in the fat, with the lid on, for 10–15 minutes. This mixture of vegetables is called a mirepoix, and is not served with the meat—it is discarded after the cooking. Place the meat on top of the vegetables and add the liquid and herbs, then leave the dish to simmer for 2–3 hours. Serve the meat with the gravy strained and poured over it.

STEAMING

Steaming is a long, slow, moist method of cooking—the food is surrounded by steam rising from boiling water. Tough joints of meat are often steamed before they are roasted, as steaming will make them more tender. Large pieces of meat can be steamed in a steamer placed over a pan of boiling water. Small cuts of tender meat can be cooked between two heatproof plates over a pan of boiling water. Steamed meat is easily digested, and none of the flavour or food value is lost.

CASSEROLE COOKING

Casserole cooking is similar to pot roasting, but the meat is cut up and cooked in liquid and the food is usually served in the dish it was cooked in. Other ingredients—vegetables, flavourings and herbs—are added to the meat, and it is usually cooked in the oven. This method of cooking requires very little attention and is ideal for both tender and tough cuts of meat, though the latter take longer to cook.

CARVING MEAT

Keep your knives sharp for efficient carving. A steel, for sharpening your knives, and a carving fork which has a guard are also essential pieces of equipment.

LEG OF LAMB

This method is simple, and gives a high yield of sliced meat. Wrap a cloth or napkin around the bone or handle of the leg. Hold the leg by the handle and rest it on a carving plate at an angle of 45°, with the meatier side uppermost. Starting midway on the joint, slice the meat down at an oblique angle. Slice down again at an opposite oblique angle and remove the wedge shaped piece of meat. Continue slicing down each side of the cut. Slices should be about 3 mm (⅛ in) thick. Keep slicing until you reach the leg bone. Turn the leg over and repeat the process.

LOIN OF LAMB

Lie the joint on its side. Place your carving fork firmly in the joint and slice straight down between the bones, into thick slices.

ROLLED RIB AND ROLLED SIRLOIN OF BEEF

Method 1: Using a fork with a safety guard, hold the joint flat on the carving plate. Slice meat across the grain towards the fork.

Method 2: Hold the joint on its side with a fork. Slice downwards, towards the carving plate.

* BEEF BOURGUIGNON *

2 tablespoons flour
1 kg (2 lb) stewing beef,
  chuck, blade or shin, diced
90 g (3 oz) butter
1 tablespoon tomato paste
2 garlic cloves, crushed
750 ml (3 cups) burgundy
625 ml (2½ cups) beef stock
  (see page 378)
salt and pepper, to taste
1 bouquet garni
60 g (2 oz) pickled pork or
  bacon, diced
12 small onions
2 carrots, sliced
12 button mushrooms
chopped parsley, to garnish

serves 6

Preheat oven to 165°C (330°F). Brown flour in a saucepan on medium heat for a few minutes until golden brown. Sprinkle diced beef with flour, then fry in a large pot with the butter for 5 minutes. Add tomato paste and garlic and cook for a further 5 minutes. Add burgundy and stock, season lightly with salt and pepper and add bouquet garni.

Cover and cook in the oven for 2½–3 hours, or until tender.

In a frying pan, fry pickled pork or bacon lightly. Add onions and carrots and cook over a moderate heat until evenly browned. Add pork or bacon and the mushrooms to the pot about 15 minutes before cooking is finished. Adjust consistency and seasoning if necessary and serve hot, sprinkled with chopped parsley.

Note: The traditional recipe has 2 tablespoons of brandy added in the final stage along with the mushrooms.

* BEEF STROGANOFF *

90 g (3 oz) butter
1 large onion, thinly sliced
250 g (8 oz) mushrooms,
    peeled and sliced
750 g (1½ lb) fillet steak,
    trimmed of fat and cut into
    thin strips
1½ teaspoons salt
freshly ground black pepper,
    to taste
pinch of nutmeg
300 g (1¼ cups) sour cream
parsley, chopped, to garnish

serves 4

Melt 60 g (2 oz) butter in a heavy frying pan and sauté the onion until soft. Add mushrooms and cook for 5 minutes. Place mixture in a bowl and keep warm.

Melt remaining butter in pan and quickly brown beef strips on all sides. Do this stage in two lots unless you have a very large frying pan. Take pan off the heat and add onion, mushrooms, salt, pepper and nutmeg. Stir well to blend, then replace pan over a medium heat and pour in sour cream. Stir gently until heated through. Do not allow sauce to boil.

Serve with boiled rice, cooked cabbage or coleslaw (see page 56).

* BOILED CORNED SILVERSIDE OR BRISKET *

1.5–2 kg (3–4 lb) piece
  corned silverside
  or brisket, rinsed
1 tablespoon brown sugar
12 whole black peppercorns
1 bay leaf
1 tablespoon vinegar
boiled carrots and onions and
  parsley sprigs, to garnish

serves 6–8

Place silverside in a deep saucepan and cover with cold water. Add remaining ingredients. Bring to simmering point and cook, covered, for 2 hours.

Garnish with carrots and onions and sprigs of parsley, and serve with white sauce (see page 377).

Note: Corned silverside can also be served cold. Allow to cool in the cooking liquid, and when cold, wrap in plastic clingwrap or aluminium foil and store in the refrigerator.

* BRAISED LAMB SHANKS *

2 tablespoons olive oil
4 lamb shanks
1 onion, chopped
1 clove garlic (optional),
   crushed
1 carrot, diced
½ cup celery, diced
1 cup skinned, chopped
   tomatoes or tinned
   tomatoes
1 teaspoon salt
¼ teaspoon freshly ground
   black pepper
½ teaspoon sugar
60 ml (¼ cup) beef stock (see
   page 378), or water
1 teaspoon Worcestershire
   sauce

serves 4

Heat oil in a frying pan and brown lamb shanks, over a moderately high heat. Pour off most of the oil and reduce heat. Add onion, garlic (if used), carrot and celery and cook until onion is soft. Stir in tomatoes, salt, pepper, sugar, stock and Worcestershire sauce. Spoon some of the vegetable mixture over the shanks. Place a lid on the pan and simmer for 2 hours, or until tender. Adjust flavour before serving.

Serve with mashed potatoes (see page 111) and steamed vegetables.

* CHILLI CON CARNE *

2 tablespoon olive oil
1 large onion, chopped
1 green capsicum (bell
  pepper), seeds and pith
  removed and chopped
1 stick celery, chopped
1 tablespoon chilli powder
  (optional)
½ teaspoon salt
pinch of cayenne pepper
2 teaspoons paprika
500 g (1 lb) minced or diced
  beef
250 g (8 oz) tomatoes or
  625 ml (2½ cups) tomato
  pulp
250 g (8 oz) cooked kidney
  beans or soaked and cooked
  haricot beans
150 ml (⅔ cup) water

serves 4

Heat oil in a saucepan. Add onion, capsicum and celery and fry until just tender, then add other ingredients. Bring just to the boil, then lower the heat and cook gently for about 55 minutes (for minced meat) or 1¼ hours (for diced meat). Stir halfway through cooking, and add a little more water if necessary.

Note: Some people like to add 60 g (2 oz) cooked rice to the recipe.

* FILLET MIGNON *

4 bacon rashers, rind
 removed
4 slices of fillet steak, 3.5 cm
 (2½ in) thick
salt and freshly ground black
 pepper, to taste
parsley butter (see page 366)

serves 4

Wrap a bacon rasher around each fillet and secure with toothpick. Preheat grill to hot and brush rack with oil. Place fillet under grill rack 8 cm (3¼ in) below heat. Grill for 3–4 minutes on each side for rare steak, 2 minutes longer each side for medium rare steak. Turn fillets gently so you don't pierce the meat and let the juices escape. Season with salt and pepper and serve immediately.

Garnish with parsley butter and serve immediately with roast potatoes.

* IRISH STEW *

1 kg (2 lb) potatoes, peeled
salt and pepper, to taste
1 kg (2 lb) lamb neck chops,
   trimmed of fat
500 g (1 lb) white onions,
   thickly sliced
bunch of herbs (parsley,
   thyme, rosemary)
1 bay leaf
625 ml (½ cup) beef stock
   (see page 378)
1 tablespoon extra parsley,
   finely chopped, to garnish

serves 5–6

Preheat oven to 165°C (330°F). Cut 3–4 potatoes into thick slices and cut remaining potatoes in halves.

Place sliced potatoes in an ovenproof casserole dish and season with salt and pepper. Cover with meat, then add onions and halved potatoes, and season again. Add herbs, bay leaf and stock.

Cover casserole dish and cook in the oven for 2–2½, hours or until meat is tender. Remove herbs and bay leaf from casserole and sprinkle with chopped parsley before serving.

* LAMB SHANKS *

6 lamb shanks
4 tablespoons olive oil
2 medium onions, diced
2 carrots, julienned
4 cloves garlic
2 tablespoons sugar
250 ml (1 cup) white
   vinegar
1 x 440 g (14 oz) can
   tomatoes, diced
250 ml (1 cup) red wine
2 tablespoons Worcestershire
   sauce
2 tablespoons sesame seeds
2 tablespoons honey
75 g (2½ oz) macadamia
   nuts, crushed
salt and freshly ground black
   pepper, to taste
bunch of fresh coriander,
   finely chopped

serves 6

Preheat oven to 150–180°C (300–350°F). Brown lamb shanks in a frying pan with 2 tablespoons of oil, then place in a casserole dish.

Heat remaining oil in a frying pan. Add onions and carrots and fry with garlic. When they start to brown, add sugar and vinegar. Lower heat and simmer uncovered for 15 minutes, so that mixture reduces.

Add tomatoes to mixture. Bring to the boil and add red wine, Worcestershire sauce and sesame seeds. Stir in honey, macadamia nuts and salt and pepper. Transfer mixture to the casserole dish, making sure it covers the lamb shanks. Sprinkle with coriander.

Cover the casserole dish with foil and cook in the oven for at least 2 hours. The longer it cooks, the more tender the lamb is.

* LESLEY'S MAGIC RISSOLES *

1 egg
60 ml (¼ cup) milk
750 g (1½ lb) fine mince
   meat
60 g (2 oz) breadcrumbs
1 tablespoon red wine
1 carrot, grated
1 zucchini, grated
1 onion, grated
1 teaspoon soy sauce
dash of Worcestershire sauce
60 g (2 oz) flour
1 tablespoon butter

serves 4

Beat egg and milk together in a large bowl. Add mince and all other ingredients except flour and butter and mix well.

Spread flour onto a cutting board. Form meat mixture into balls and roll in flour. Then flatten (with a spatula or knife) into rissoles and place on greaseproof paper. Continue until all mixture has been used.

Heat butter in a frying pan over a low heat. Place rissoles in the frying pan and cook for 5 minutes, or until the bottom is golden brown, then turn and continue to cook for 10 minutes or until golden brown on the other side and cooked through.

Serve with vegetables and mashed potato (see page 111).

* MEATLOAF *

750 g (1½ lb) minced beef
45 g (1½ oz) breadcrumbs
1 onion, grated
½ cup carrot, grated
2 tablespoons capsicum (bell
  pepper)(optional), seeds
  and pith removed and
  finely chopped
60 ml (¼ cup) tomato purée
60 ml (¼ cup) milk
1 egg, beaten
2 tablespoons parsley,
  chopped
½ teaspoon mixed herbs
1½ teaspoons salt
freshly ground black pepper,
  to taste
chopped parsley, to garnish

serves 4–6

Preheat oven to 180°C (350°F). Place minced beef in a large bowl. In another bowl, blend together the breadcrumbs, onion, carrot, capsicum (if used), tomato purée and milk. Stir in egg, herbs and salt and pepper. Combine this mixture with the minced beef.

Spoon meat mixture into a greased standard-sized loaf tin and bake in the oven for 1 hour. Drain off liquid, unmould onto a warm serving platter and serve garnished with parsley and accompanied by steamed vegetables and potatoes.

Variation:
Tomato–Cheese Loaf: Unmould meatloaf as above, lay slices of tomato and cheese on top and return to the oven until cheese melts and browns slightly.

* MINUTE STEAKS *

8 pieces fillet steak, 2.5 cm
  (1 in) thick, trimmed of fat
salt and black pepper, to taste
250 g (8 oz) butter for frying

Steak Champignon
500 g (1 lb) mushrooms,
  sliced
315 ml (1¼ cups) fresh
  cream

Steak Diane
4 tablespoons parsley, finely
  chopped
16 cloves garlic, crushed
8 teaspoons Worcestershire
  sauce

Paprika Steak
pinch of paprika
8 tablespoons brandy

serves 8

Pound steaks with a meat mallet until they are 5 mm (¼ in) thick. Rub with salt and pepper.

Melt 30 g (1 oz) butter in a frying pan for each steak. When butter is sizzling, add steak and fry for 1 minute on each side. Serve each steak as it is cooked, and spoon over the pan juices.

Variations:
Steak Champignon: Add 60 g (2 oz) mushrooms to pan as you cook steak. When turning steak, add 1 tablespoon cream. Lift out steaks and mushrooms. Heat pan juices for 10 seconds over high heat, stirring continuously. Pour over steaks and serve.

Steak Diane: As steak starts to sizzle, sprinkle with chopped parsley and 1 crushed clove garlic. As steak is turned, add 1 teaspoon Worcestershire sauce, a little more parsley and 1 more crushed clove of garlic. Cook for 1 minute on second side and serve.

Paprika Steak: Sprinkle both sides of steak with paprika before cooking. Once steaks are cooked, add 1 tablespoon of brandy to pan for each steak, just before serving. Ignite and serve.

* MOUSSAKA *

4 tablespoons olive oil
2 onions, finely chopped
2 cloves garlic, crushed
500 g (1 lb) lamb
  forequarter, chopped or
  minced
185 g (6 oz) mushrooms,
  chopped
500 g (1 lb) tomatoes,
  skinned, seeded and
  chopped
2 tablespoons tomato paste
150 ml (2/3 cup) beef stock
  (see page 378)
2 medium-sized eggplants,
  cut into 1 cm (1/2 in) slices
125 g (4 oz) plain (all-
  purpose) flour
salt and pepper, to taste
90 g (3 oz) parmesan cheese,
  grated
1 tablespoon parsley, chopped

serves 6

Preheat oven to 200°C (400°F). Heat 1 tablespoon olive oil in a large saucepan till hot, then sauté onion and garlic until soft, but not coloured. Add lamb and fry until lightly browned. Add mushrooms and tomatoes and cook for 5 minutes. Add tomato paste and stock. Cook for a further 5 minutes.

Roll eggplant slices in flour. Heat remaining oil in a frying pan, and fry eggplant slices on both sides. Drain on absorbent paper. Line the base of an ovenproof casserole dish with slices of eggplant. Pour over some of the lamb mixture, season with salt and pepper and sprinkle with parsley. Cover with another layer of eggplant and repeat the process until casserole dish is full, finishing with a layer of eggplant. Sprinkle with parmesan cheese and cook in the oven until golden brown—approximately 10–15 minutes. Serve sprinkled with chopped parsley.

Variation: Before adding the parmesan cheese, pour over a layer of béchamel sauce (see page 351) and cook in the oven for approximately 15–20 minutes.

* PORK WITH MARSALA *

500–750 g (1–1½ lb) pork
  fillets, trimmed of fat
flour, seasoned with salt and
  freshly ground black pepper,
  for coating
3 tablespoons olive oil
salt and freshly ground black
  pepper, to taste
1 tablespoon water
2 tablespoons plain (all-
  purpose) flour
125 ml (½ cup) marsala (see
  glossary)
30 g (1 oz) butter

serves 4

Slice pork lengthways, almost through, so they form a butterfly fillet. Lay fillets open between 2 sheets of plastic clingwrap, and flatten with a meat mallet. Cut meat into pieces about 10 x 5 cm (4 x 2 in). Pound again until very thin, taking care not to break the slices. Dust lightly with seasoned flour.

Heat oil in a pan and brown meat for 2 minutes on each side over a high heat. Sprinkle lightly with salt and generously with pepper, then remove meat from the pan and arrange slices overlapping on a warm serving dish. Keep warm.

Add water to pan, then add flour and stir in, scraping up the crusty meat and flour leftovers. Pour in marsala and stir until sauce is thickened and smooth, then add butter. When butter is melted, pour hot sauce over meat and serve.

* POT ROAST *

3 tablespoons butter
1.5–2 kg (3–4 lb) corner
   piece topside steak
2 large carrots, peeled and
   cut into chunks
2 large parsnips, peeled and
   cut into chunks
5–6 onions, peeled and cut
   into chunks
salt and freshly ground black
   pepper, to taste
180 ml (⅔ cup) water

serves 5–6

Heat butter in a large flameproof casserole dish (use one that has a tight-fitting lid) and brown meat evenly on all sides. Remove meat from dish and set aside. Brown vegetables in remaining fat, remove from dish and set aside.

Put meat back in casserole dish, season with salt and pepper and add 2 tablespoons boiling water. Cover casserole with greased paper or aluminium foil and put the lid on. Cook over a gentle heat for 2½ hours, or until meat is tender, adding 2 tablespoons boiling water to casserole every 30 minutes.
Add vegetables 1½ hours before cooking time is completed.

Serve with new potatoes and gravy from casserole.

* ROAST LEG OF LAMB *

1 x 1.5 kg (3 lb) leg of lamb
salt, to taste
freshly ground black pepper,
  to taste
2 cloves garlic, sliced
2–3 sprigs fresh rosemary

serves 4–6

Preheat oven to 165°C (330°F).

Place lamb in a roasting pan and rub the meat with salt and pepper. Make cuts into meat and press slices of garlic inside. Place sprigs of rosemary on top of lamb.

Roast lamb in the oven for 1 hour and 40 minutes. Basting is not required unless the lamb is very young and has little fat. Season with salt after roasting and let the joint stand in a warm place for 15 minutes before carving.

Serve with roast vegetables, gravy, mint sauce (see page 366) or mint jelly.

* RACK OF LAMB *

1 rib rack of 6 lamb cutlets,
  trimmed of fat
pinch of salt
mint jelly or mint sauce (see
  page 366)

serves 3

Preheat oven to 165°C (325°F). Rub lamb with salt.
Place lamb on a rack in a roasting pan and cook in the
oven for about 45 minutes. Carve (on a board) into 6
cutlets. Place 2 cutlets on each plate, with frills placed
on each bone. Serve with mint jelly or mint sauce.

* ROAST BEEF *

1 x 1.5 kg (3 lb) rolled
  sirloin of beef
salt and freshly ground black
  pepper, to taste
butter or olive oil, for
  roasting

serves 6

Preheat oven to 165°C (330°F). Rub meat with salt
and pepper and place in a roasting pan, fat side up. If
the joint has little fat, add 1–2 tablespoons butter or
oil to the pan. Place beef in the oven and cook for 2
hours.

Remove roast beef to a hot carving platter and leave
to stand in a warm place for 15–30 minutes before
carving. This makes it easier to carve the meat.

Serve with Yorkshire Pudding (see page 346), roast
vegetables (pumpkin or parsnip), and with gravy
(see page 357), horseradish cream (see page 360) or
mustard.

* ROAST PORK *

1 x 3 kg (6 lb) loin leg of
  pork
salt, to taste
apple sauce (see page 350),
  to serve

serves 8–12

Preheat oven to 245°C (480°F). Rub pork with salt
and place in a roasting pan. Cook pork in oven for
30 minutes to crisp crackling, then reduce heat to
moderately slow (165°C/330°F) and cook for 3 hours.
Continue to baste throughout cooking time.

When pork is cooked, place in a carving tray and
keep warm. Make gravy from pan juices.

Serve roast pork with apple sauce, roast potatoes
and roast vegetables.

* ROAST PRIME RIB OF BEEF WITH YORKSHIRE PUDDING *

*1 x 5 kg (10 lb) prime rib of
  beef on the bone*
salt, to taste
gravy, to serve (see page 357)
*horseradish cream (see page
  360)*
*Yorkshire Pudding (see page
  346)*

serves 12–15

Preheat oven to 165°C (330°F). Rub beef with salt and place in a roasting pan. Place in the oven and cook for 3 hours. Remove from oven and allow to stand in a warm place for 30 minutes. This helps retain the juices and makes the meat easier to carve. While the meat is setting, prepare gravy.

Carve meat and serve with horseradish sauce, Yorkshire Pudding and gravy.

* SESAME LAMB *

1 tablespoon oil
2 medium onions, diced
1 carrot, diced
1 parsnip, diced
2 teaspoons garlic, chopped
3 bacon rashers, diced
1 kg lamb leg meat, diced
250 ml (1 cup) red wine
1 teaspoon mixed herbs
3 bay leaves
salt and freshly ground black
   pepper, to taste
8 mushrooms, sliced or diced
fresh coriander leaves,
   chopped, to taste
2 tablespoons sesame seeds

serves 6

Heat oil in a frying pan and fry onion, carrot, parsnip and garlic for 5 minutes. Add bacon and cook for a few more minutes. Add lamb, red wine, mixed herbs, bay leaves and salt and pepper. Bring mixture to the boil (add a little water if necessary), then reduce heat and simmer for 30 minutes. Add mushrooms, coriander and sesame seeds and simmer for a further 15 minutes.

Serve with rice or potatoes. Garnish with a little fresh coriander.

Note: You can 'heat up' the dish by adding a small amount of hot chilli sauce.

* SHEPHERD'S PIE *

1 tablespoon olive oil
1 onion, finely chopped
2 tomatoes, skinned and
  chopped
375 g (12 oz) beef mince,
  cooked
good pinch of mixed herbs
salt and pepper, to taste
315 ml (1¼ cups) beef stock
  (see page 378)
500 g (1 lb) mashed potato
  (see page 111)
30 g (1 oz) butter

serves 4

Preheat oven to 200°C (375°F). In a frying pan, heat olive oil and fry onion for 3 minutes. Add tomatoes and meat and heat together for 2–3 minutes. Stir in herbs, seasoning and stock—add less stock if you desire a thicker consistency.

Put meat mixture into a pie dish and cover with mashed potato. Use a fork to score the edges, or create any other design you like. Dot tiny pieces of butter around on the potato to help it brown. Bake in the centre of the oven until the top is crisp and brown.

* SPICY LAMB CURRY *

1 medium onion, chopped
2 cloves garlic, crushed
¼ teaspoon chilli powder
60 ml (¼ cup) lemon juice
1 tablespoon curry powder
½ teaspoon celery salt (see
  glossary)
½ teaspoon ground ginger
1.5 kg (3 lb) lamb chops, cut
  into 2.5 cm (1 in) cubes
2 tablespoons olive oil
2 medium onions, chopped
2 cloves garlic, crushed
½ teaspoon mustard seeds
  (see glossary)
½ teaspoon cumin
1 teaspoon turmeric
1 teaspoon paprika
½ teaspoon garam masala
  (see glossary)
1 medium tomato, peeled
  and chopped
250 ml (1 cup) chicken stock
  (see page 380)
125 ml (½ cup) coconut
  cream

serves 6

Combine onion, garlic, chilli powder, lemon juice, curry powder, celery salt, ground ginger and lamb cubes in a bowl, and stir until lamb is evenly coated. Cover, and refrigerate for 1 hour.

Preheat oven to 180°C (350°F). Heat oil in a large saucepan and add onions and garlic. Sauté for 1 minute. Add lamb and cook, stirring, until browned. Add mustard seeds, cumin, turmeric, paprika, garam masala, tomato and chicken stock, and cook for 5 minutes. Spoon into a large ovenproof dish and cover.

Bake in the oven for 1½ hours, or until tender. Stir in coconut cream just before serving. Serve with boiled or steamed rice.

* STEAK DIANE *

4 slices of fillet steak cut
  2.5 cm (1 in) thick
30 g (1 oz) butter
2 cloves garlic, crushed
salt and freshly ground black
  pepper, to taste
1 tablespoon tomato sauce
1 teaspoon Worcestershire
  sauce
60 ml (¼ cup) water
1 teaspoon cornflour, mixed
  with a little cold water

serves 4

Slit steaks horizontally through to the centre and open out meat to create a butterfly fillet. Flatten steaks with the side of a meat mallet to 5 mm (¼ in) thickness.

Melt half the butter in a heavy frying pan, add 1 crushed garlic clove and fry the steaks quickly—about 40 seconds on each side for rare steak and 1 minute each side for medium steak. Add remaining butter and garlic to the pan when cooking the rest of the steaks (most frying pans will probably hold only two steaks at a time). Season cooked steaks with salt and pepper and keep aside on a warm platter.

Add sauces and water to frying pan and stir into pan juices over a medium heat. Thicken with cornflour paste and bring to the boil. Pour sauce over steaks.

Serve with new potatoes and a tossed green salad.

* STEAK AND KIDNEY PIE *

2 sheep's kidneys, skinned,
   halved and cored
1 teaspoon salt
freshly ground black pepper,
   to taste
2 tablespoons plain (all-
   purpose) flour
2 tablespoons butter
500 g (1 lb) casserole steak
   (chuck, blade, flank, skirt
   or round), trimmed and
   cut into 1 cm (½ in) cubes
125 ml (½ cup) water
375 g (12 oz) flaky pastry or
   puff pastry
2 tablespoons parsley,
   chopped
1 egg, beaten

serves 4

Cut kidney into small pieces. Season flour with salt and pepper, then coat meat and kidneys with flour.

Melt butter in a heavy saucepan (use one that has a lid) over a moderate heat and brown steak and kidney, stirring continuously. Add water, cover tightly and simmer gently for 1 hour. Stir in parsley, then leave to cool.

Roll out pastry to a circle that is 2.5 cm (1 in) larger than the top of your pie dish. Cut a strip 1 cm (½ in) wide off the edge and place it on dampened rim of dish. Brush it with cold water. Spoon steak and kidney into dish. Place remaining pastry on top of mixture and press edges of pastry onto pastry rim to seal. Trim off excess pastry and decorate edge by flaking and fluting with the back of a fork. Glaze pie with egg and cut a cross on top about 2 cm deep.

Bake in the oven for 20 minutes, then reduce heat to moderately slow (165°C/325°F) and bake for a further 20 minutes.

* SWEET AND SOUR PORK *

500 g (1 lb) pork fillets (pork
   chops can be used), cut into
   thin strips
3 tablespoons cornflour or
   plain (all-purpose) flour
olive oil for frying

Sweet and Sour Sauce
250 ml (1 cup) chicken stock
   (see page 380)
125 ml (½ cup)
   pineapple juice
2 tablespoons vinegar
1 cup canned pineapple
   (shredded or cubed)
1 carrot, finely sliced
1 cup green capsicum (bell
   pepper), sliced
salt and freshly ground black
   pepper, to taste
2 tablespoons cornflour
6 shallots, finely chopped
2 teaspoons soy sauce

serves 6

Coat pork with cornflour. Heat oil in a frying pan and
fry meat for 20 minutes, or until golden brown and
thoroughly cooked. Drain meat well and keep hot.

To make sauce, place stock, pineapple juice,
vinegar, pineapple, carrot, celery, salt and pepper
into a saucepan. Bring to the boil, then reduce heat
and simmer for 10 minutes, or until vegetables are
cooked, but firm.

In a cup, blend cornflour to a paste with a little
water and add to pineapple mixture. Boil for
2 minutes, or until thickened to desired consistency.
Just before serving, add shallots, soy sauce and pork
and stir to combine.

Serve on a bed of steamed rice.

* TASTY ROAST BEEF *

2 teaspoons dry mustard (see
  glossary)
2 tablespoons plain (all-
  purpose) flour
1 teaspoon salt
¼ teaspoon freshly ground
  black pepper
1 teaspoon brown sugar
1 x 1.5–2 kg (3–4 lb) rolled
  rib of beef
2 tablespoons olive oil
250 ml (1 cup) beer
chives, finely chopped, to
  serve

serves 6

Preheat oven to 220°C (420°F). Mix together the
mustard, flour, salt, pepper and brown sugar and rub
all over meat, using a skewer to force some down into
the centre of the joint.

Heat oil in a roasting pan, put meat in and
place pan in the oven to sear the meat. Turn after
5 minutes. Pour beer over beef. Reduce heat to
moderate (180°C/350°F) and roast for 1½–2 hours,
basting occasionally.

Serve with vegetables. Brush vegetables with olive
oil and bake in the oven for 25–30 minutes or until
tender.

* T-BONE STEAK *

4 t-bone steaks
olive oil
8 large mushrooms, whole
4 medium tomatoes, halved
salt and freshly ground black
   pepper, to taste

serves 4

Allow steaks to stand at room temperature for 30 minutes before cooking. Cut fat around edge in two or three places to prevent steak curling.

Preheat grill until hot. Place steaks on grill rack and brush lean surface of meat lightly with oil. Grill steaks for 2 minutes on either side to seal surface of meat, turning with tongs or two spoons to avoid piercing the meat and letting the juices escape. Reduce heat and grill for a further 4–5 minutes on each side.

Place mushrooms on grill rack and cook for 2 minutes, then add tomatoes and grill for a further 3 minutes. Turn mushrooms and tomatoes once during grilling time. Season steak, mushrooms and tomatoes with salt and pepper before serving.

Serve with a tossed green salad and some flavoured butter.

* VEAL CORDON BLEU *

8 medium-sized veal steaks,
  cut from leg
4 thin slices ham (about size
  of steaks)
4 thin slices gruyère cheese
seasoned flour (see glossary),
  for coating
1 egg, beaten with
  1 tablespoon water
breadcrumbs, for coating
oil, for frying
lemon wedges, to garnish

serves 4

Flatten veal steaks between two sheets of plastic clingwrap by beating with the side of a meat mallet or a rolling pin. Put the steaks in pairs, so that pieces in a pair are of a similar size. Place a slice of ham and a slice of cheese between each pair of steaks, keeping ham and cheese 5 mm (¼ in) in from edge of veal all round. Beat edges to seal. Coat veal with seasoned flour, dip carefully in egg, then coat with breadcrumbs, pressing them on firmly.

Allow to stand for 10 minutes, then heat oil in a frying pan and shallow fry veal over a moderate heat until light golden brown. Turn carefully and brown other side. It will take about 5 minutes to completely cook the veal. Drain on absorbent paper and serve piping hot.

Garnish with lemon wedges and serve with boiled new potatoes and vegetables.

Note: If cheese leaks out of the steak and causes spitting, place a slice of potato in the pan—it will absorb moisture.

* VEAL WITH MOZZARELLA *

750 g (1½ lb) veal steak,
  thinly sliced
seasoned flour (see glossary)
1 egg, beaten with 60 ml
  (¼ cup) water
1 cup fine breadcrumbs
  mixed with ¼ cup
  parmesan cheese, grated
olive oil, for frying
2 tablespoons extra olive oil
2 cloves garlic, crushed
1 onion, finely chopped
1 x 470 g (15 oz) can
  tomatoes, peeled
3 tablespoons tomato paste
¼ teaspoon dried thyme
½ teaspoon caster (superfine)
  sugar
salt and freshly ground black
  pepper, to taste
250 g (8 oz) mozzarella
  cheese, thinly sliced

serves 4

Preheat oven to 180°C (350°F). Flatten veal slices lightly, using the side of a meat mallet. Dip in seasoned flour, then in combined egg and water, and then coat with combined breadcrumbs and parmesan cheese. Press crumbs on firmly.

Heat oil in a frying pan and fry veal until golden brown on both sides. Drain on absorbent paper.

Heat extra oil in a saucepan, then add garlic and onion and sauté for 5 minutes. Add tomatoes, tomato paste, thyme, sugar and salt and pepper. Cover, and simmer for 10 minutes.

Pour one-third of tomato mixture into an ovenproof casserole dish. Arrange veal on top, cover with cheese and pour over remaining sauce. Cook, uncovered, in the oven for 30–35 minutes.

Serve with a tossed green salad.

* VIENNA SCHNITZEL *

500 g (1 lb) thinly cut veal
  steak, cut from leg
1 clove garlic, crushed
  (optional)
1 tablespoon lemon juice
salt and freshly ground black
  pepper, to taste
plain (all-purpose) flour, for
  coating
1 egg, beaten with
  1 tablespoon water
breadcrumbs, for coating
olive oil, for frying
hard-boiled egg, anchovy
  fillets, capers, lemon slices
  and parsley, to garnish

serves 4

Flatten veal between two pieces of plastic clingwrap, using the side of a meat mallet or rolling pin. Cut skin on edges to prevent curling during cooking. Lay veal on a plate and set aside.

Mix garlic (optional) with lemon juice and brush onto veal. Season with salt and pepper and allow to stand for 30 minutes. Dip each slice of veal into flour, then egg, and finally breadcrumbs, pressing them firmly on to coat veal completely. Refrigerate for 1 hour.

Heat oil in a frying pan and shallow fry veal steaks over a moderate heat for about 2 minutes on either side, or until golden brown. Lift veal onto absorbent paper to drain, then place on a hot serving platter.

Garnish each schnitzel with a slice of hard-boiled egg and top with a rolled anchovy fillet, a few capers, lemon slice and parsley.

Serve with boiled new potatoes, sauerkraut and a tossed salad.

Sweets
& desserts

* APPLE CRUMBLE *

6 cooking apples, peeled,
  cored and sliced
3 cloves
125 ml (½ cup) honey
125 g (4 oz) plain (all-
  purpose) wholemeal flour
100 g (3½ oz) oatmeal
30 g (1 oz) wheat germ (see
  glossary)
¼ teaspoon salt
90 g (3 oz) raw sugar
185 g (6 oz) butter
whipped cream or vanilla
  custard sauce (see page
  376), for serving

serves 8

Preheat oven to 200°C (400°F). Place apples in an ovenproof dish. Add cloves and pour over honey.

Place flour, oatmeal, wheat germ, salt and sugar in a bowl. Rub in butter until mixture is crumbly, then spread mixture over apples.

Bake in the oven for 1 hour, or until top is golden brown. Serve with vanilla custard sauce.

* BAKED APPLES *

8 prunes, stoned and chopped
2 tablespoons raisins
4 cooking apples, cored
4 tablespoons honey
30 g (1 oz) butter
4 tablespoons water
vanilla custard sauce (see
  page 376), for serving

serves 8

Preheat oven to 180°C (350°F). In a bowl, combine prunes with raisins. Stuff apples with prunes and raisins and place in a baking dish. Pour honey over apples and dot with butter. Add water to baking dish.

Bake in the oven for ¾–1 hour, or until apples are tender. Serve hot with vanilla custard sauce.

*BAKED CUSTARD *

2 large eggs
60 g (2 oz) caster (superfine)
 sugar
500 ml (2 cups) milk,
 scalded
1 teaspoon vanilla
⅛ teaspoon salt
1 teaspoon nutmeg, grated

serves 4–6

Preheat oven to 180°C (350°F). In a bowl, beat eggs lightly. Add sugar and combine, then add scalded milk, slowly, until sugar is dissolved. Add vanilla and stir through, then add salt and stir through.

Pour into a large pie dish or ovenproof dish. Sprinkle a little grated nutmeg on top, set in a shallow tin or dish half full of water and bake in the oven for 20–30 minutes, or until a knife pier-cing the custard comes out clean.

Serve hot or cold.

* BANANA CAKE *

125 g (4 oz) butter
125 g (4 oz) caster sugar
1 teaspoon vanilla
2 small eggs
3 small ripe bananas,
  mashed
250 g (8 oz) self-raising
  flour, sifted
1 teaspoon bicarbonate of
  soda (baking soda) (see
  glossary)
1 tablespoon milk
250 ml (1 cup) fresh cream,
  whipped
lemon frosting (see page 348)

serves 6–8

Preheat oven to 200°C (400°F). In a bowl, cream butter, caster sugar and vanilla thoroughly. Add eggs, one at a time, beating well after each addition. Add bananas to mixture and combine well. Add half flour and fold in lightly.

Dissolve bicarbonate of soda in milk and add to mixture. Stir in gently. Add remaining flour and mix well.

Pour mixture into two greased and floured 20 cm (8 in) cake tins and bake in the oven for about 25 minutes. The cake is ready when a wooden skewer inserted into the centre comes out clean.

When cold, join cakes with cream, ice with lemon frosting.

✱ BREAD AND BUTTER PUDDING ✱

Custard

2 eggs
*1 tablespoon caster
   (superfine) sugar*
*150 ml (⅔ cup) milk,
   warmed*
pinch of nutmeg, grated

*2 large or 4 small slices of
   bread*
butter
60 g (2 oz) dried fruit
extra sugar

serves 4

To make custard, beat eggs in a bowl with a fork. Beat in sugar and milk; the milk must not boil, or it will curdle the eggs. Pour into a greased pie dish or basin and top with grated nutmeg. Put the basin into a steamer over very hot water and cook steadily for about 1½ hours. Make sure that the water does not boil—this will curdle the custard.

Preheat oven to 180°C (350°F). Remove crusts from bread, and butter bread thinly. Cut into neat squares or triangles and arrange in a pie dish. Add dried fruit and pour egg custard over the top. Allow to stand for 30 minutes. Sprinkle the top with a little sugar and bake for 1 hour in the oven. If the pudding appears to be cooking too quickly after 45 minutes, reduce to 130°C (265°F).

* CARROT CAKE *

125 g (4 oz) self-raising flour
180 g (6 oz) brown sugar,
  packed tightly
2 teaspoons cinnamon
2 cups carrot, finely grated
½ cup raisins, chopped
2 eggs
125 ml (½ cup) olive oil
¼ cup walnuts, chopped

Frosting
30 g (1 oz) cream cheese
30 g (1 oz) butter
100 g (3½ oz) icing sugar
1 teaspoon lemon juice

serves 6–8

In a bowl, mix together flour, sugar, cinnamon, carrots and raisins. Add eggs and oil and combine thoroughly. Pour into a 20 cm (8 in) spring-form cake tin lined with greaseproof paper and cook medium–high for 8 minutes until just cooked. Let cake stand for 5 minutes.

To make frosting, beat cream cheese and butter in a bowl until smooth; for best results, use an electric mixer. Gradually mix in icing sugar and lemon juice.

Allow cake to cool then top with frosting and walnuts.

Note: This is a microwave recipe.

* CHEESECAKE *

Crust
1 x 225 g (7 oz) packet plain
  sweet biscuits
125 g (4 oz) butter

Filling
250 g (8 oz) cream cheese
80 ml (⅓ cup) lemon juice
1 x 410 g (13½ oz) can
  condensed milk (see
  glossary)
whipped cream, to garnish
lemon rind, thinly sliced, to
  garnish

serves 10

To make the crust, put biscuits in a plastic bag and seal the top with an elastic band or twist tie. Using a rolling pin, crush the biscuits in the bag—you will need to roll again and again. Pour biscuit crumbs into a bowl.

Melt butter in a saucepan over medium heat, then pour melted butter over biscuit crumbs and mix thoroughly. Tip biscuit mixture into a spring-form cake tin and spread it out, then press it down firmly with the back of a spoon. Make sure you press some up the sides as well. The biscuit crust should be about 5 mm (¼ in) thick all over. Put the cake tin in the refrigerator for 20 minutes while you prepare the filling.

To make the filling, put the cream cheese in a bowl and mash it up with a fork. Add lemon juice and condensed milk and beat with an egg beater until the mixture is smooth. Pour cheese mixture into the pie dish and smooth over gently with a spoon. Put the cheesecake in the refrigerator and leave to set for at least 4 hours.

When ready to serve, garnish with whipped cream and thinly sliced lemon rind.

* CHOC-COFFEE SURPRISES *

125 g (4 oz) butter
180 g (6 oz) icing
  (confectioners') sugar
1 teaspoon vanilla
1 teaspoon hot water
2 teaspoons instant coffee
  powder
60 g (2 oz) caster (superfine)
  sugar
80 ml (⅓ cup) water
140 g (4½ oz) desiccated
  coconut
2 teaspoons vanilla
1 egg white, lightly beaten
125 g (4 oz) dark chocolate,
  chopped
30 g (1 oz) copha, melted
  (see glossary)

makes 25

In a bowl, cream butter, icing sugar and vanilla until light and fluffy. In a cup, combine hot water and instant coffee. Add this to butter and sugar mixture and beat well. Refrigerate until firm.

Roll teaspoonfuls of mixture into small balls and chill for 30 minutes.

In a saucepan, stir sugar and water over a medium heat until sugar dissolves. Bring to the boil, remove from heat and stir in coconut, vanilla and egg white. Keep stirring until well combined, then set aside to cool.

Mould about two teaspoonfuls of the coconut mixture around each coffee ball and chill.

Melt chocolate and copha together in a basin over a saucepan of hot water or in the top of a double boiler. Dip chilled balls into chocolate and copha mixture. Refrigerate for 24 hours before eating, to allow flavour to develop.

* CHOCOLATE AND DATE SLICE *

1 cup dates, chopped
125 g (4 oz) self-raising
  (self-rising) flour
250 g (8 oz) brown sugar
45 g (1½ oz) desiccated
  coconut
½ cup chocolate bits
125 g (4 oz) butter
1 tablespoon golden syrup
1 egg, beaten

serves 6–8

Preheat oven to 180°C (350°F). In a bowl, combine all the dry ingredients.

In a small saucepan, melt butter and stir in golden syrup. Cool slightly then add egg and mix. Add the melted butter mixture to the dry ingredients and mix together well.

Line a rectangular cake pan (about 30 x 20 cm/ 12 x 10 in) with baking paper (or just grease the dish) and pour mixture in. Press it flat with the back of a spoon. Bake in the oven for 20–25 minutes, or until golden brown.

Variation: Add mixed fruit and/or mixed nuts instead of all the dates, and/or ice the slice with lemon frosting (see page 348) when it has cooled.

* CHOCOLATE FUDGE *

750 g (3 cups) caster
 (superfine) sugar
1½ tablespoons cocoa
250 ml (1 cup) milk
1 tablespoon glucose syrup
 (see glossary)
20 g (⅔ oz) butter
few drops vanilla essence

makes 36 squares

Combine sugar, cocoa, milk and glucose syrup in a saucepan. Stir over a low heat until sugar is dissolved and begins to boil. Watch that it does not boil over. Continue cooking until a small amount of the fudge forms a soft ball when dropped into a glass of cold water (about 10 minutes).

Remove fudge from the heat and tip it into a large bowl. Add butter and vanilla essence and beat until the mixture is thick and creamy. Pour immediately into a greased cake tin (4.5 cm x 3 cm/11 x 7 in) and cut into small squares.

Put the fudge in the refrigerator until it is cold, then break it into squares.

* CHOCOLATE LOG *

60 ml (¼ cup) milk
625 ml (2½ cups) fresh
  cream
6 teaspoons caster (superfine)
  sugar
225 g (7 oz) plain chocolate
  biscuits

serves 6

Pour milk in one bowl and 315 ml (11 oz) cream in
another. Add 3 teaspoons sugar to cream and whip it
with an egg beater until stiff.

Dip one biscuit quickly in the milk and cover one
side of it with whipped cream. Stand the biscuit on its
edge in a long narrow loaf tin. Dip the next biscuit in
the milk, cover one side with cream and stand it right
next to the first biscuit. Continue in this way along
the plate, forming a log and using all the biscuits and
all the whipped cream.

Put the remaining cream and sugar in the bowl
and beat until thick. Spread this cream all over the
log, covering it completely. Decorate with chocolate
buttons or nuts as you wish.

Put the log in the refrigerator and leave for at least
4 hours. It tastes better if you eat it the next day. To
serve the log, cut it diagonally so that each piece is
striped.

* CHOCOLATE MOUSSE *

2 tablespoons brandy
5 eggs, separated
375 g (12 oz) good quality
  dark chocolate, chopped
300 ml (1¼ cups/1 carton)
  thickened cream

serves 8

In a small saucepan, beat brandy and egg yolks until smooth. Meanwhile, melt chocolate in a bowl over hot water, stirring until smooth. Cool chocolate, then whisk in the yolk mixture.

In another bowl, beat egg whites until they form soft peaks. In a third bowl, beat cream until stiff. Fold egg whites and cream into chocolate mixture until no streaks remain.

Spoon into 8 mousse pots or 1 large serving dish. Cover and chill for at least 3 hours, or until set.

* CHOCOLATE PUDDING *

60 g (2 oz) self-raising (self-
    rising) flour
2 tablespoons cocoa
60 g (2 oz) breadcrumbs
60 g (2 oz) butter
60 g (2 oz) caster (superfine)
    sugar
1 egg (optional)
dash of milk
few drops vanilla essence

serves 4

Sift flour and cocoa into a bowl, then add all other dry ingredients and mix thoroughly. In another bowl, beat egg (if using) and milk, then stir in vanilla essence.

Stir enough liquid into the dry mixture to give it a slightly sticky consistency. Grease and flour a bowl and put the mixture in it. Cover with greased greaseproof paper and steam or boil for about 1¾ hours.

Serve with vanilla custard sauce (see page 376).

* CHOCOLATE STRAWBERRIES *

125 g (4 oz) dark chocolate,
  chopped
125 g (4 oz) white chocolate,
  chopped
60 g (2 oz) copha (see
  glossary)
500 g (1 lb) strawberries,
  washed

serves 8

Melt the dark chocolate and half of the copha gently in a bowl over hot water, or in the top of a double boiler, then cool slightly.

Melt the white chocolate and rest of the copha gently in a bowl over hot water, or in the top of a double boiler, then cool slightly.

Hold each berry by the stem and dip it (to two-thirds of its depth) into either the dark or white chocolate mixture. Place dipped berries on a plastic-covered tray. Chill. Serve with coffee.

Note: Chocolate strawberries can be made (and kept in the refrigerator) for up to 24 hours before serving.

* CHOCOLATE WALNUT BROWNIES *

*60 g (2 oz) plain (all-
   purpose) flour*
1 tablespoon bran
*¼ teaspoon baking powder
   (see glossary)*
60 g (2 oz) walnuts, chopped
60 g (2 oz) butter
60 g (2 oz) cooking chocolate
180 g (6 oz) brown sugar
2 eggs, beaten
½ teaspoon vanilla essence

makes 16 squares

Preheat oven to 180°C (350°F). Grease a 28 x 18 cm (11 x 7 in) shallow baking tin. Cut a piece of greaseproof paper long enough to cover the sides of the tin, going a little higher than the edge of the tin. Press greaseproof paper inside the tin, cutting down into each corner so you can fold the paper round to fit.

In a bowl, mix together flour, bran, baking powder and walnuts.

In a saucepan, melt butter with chocolate and sugar. Cool slightly, then whisk in eggs and vanilla essence with a fork. Pour this into the flour mixture and mix well.

Pour mixture into the prepared tin and bake in the oven for 35 minutes, until the cake has risen and the centre springs back when lightly pressed. Leave to cool in the tin, then cut into squares.

* COCONUT MACAROONS *

2 egg whites
150 g (5 oz) caster
  (superfine) sugar
½ teaspoon cornflour
125 g (4 oz) desiccated
  coconut
vanilla or almond essence

makes 30

Preheat oven to 130°C (265°F). In a bowl, beat egg whites until they are stiff. Gradually add caster sugar, beating well after each addition. Add cornflour and fold in well.

Place mixture in an enamel, stainless steel or other heatproof bowl and beat over a saucepan of boiling water until mixture begins to cook on the bottom of the basin. Fold in the coconut and vanilla or almond essence.

Place teaspoons of the mixture onto a greased baking tray and bake in the oven for 25 minutes.

* COFFEE CAKE *

125 g (4 oz) butter
185 g (6 oz) caster
  (superfine) sugar
1 egg
½ teaspoon vanilla essence
250 g (8 oz) self-raising flour
½ teaspoon salt
185 ml (¾ cup) milk
2 tablespoons golden syrup
1 teaspoon ground cinnamon
¼ teaspoon ground nutmeg
¼ teaspoon ground cloves
½ teaspoon ground
  cinnamon

Topping
125 g (4 oz) brown sugar
60–90 g (2–3 oz) chopped
  walnuts
2 good tablespoons plain
  (all-purpose) flour
½ teaspoon ground
  cinnamon
60 g (2 oz) butter, melted

makes 12–16 squares

Preheat oven to 180°C (350°F). Cream butter and sugar in a bowl until light and fluffy. Add egg and beat well, then add vanilla essence. Sift the flour and salt together, then add to the creamed mixture alternately with the milk, a little at a time and stir until well combined. Divide mixture in half.

To one half add golden syrup and spices. Line a 23 cm (9 in) square cake tin with baking paper, and spoon mixtures alternately into the cake tin. Zigzag a spatula through the mixture to give a marbled effect.

To make topping, put brown sugar, walnuts, flour and cinnamon into a bowl, then add butter and mix well. Sprinkle mixture over dough in cake tin and bake in the oven for 30 minutes. Let cake cool, then cut into squares.

* COFFEE SLICE *

125 g (4 oz) butter
125 g (4 oz) self-raising
  (self-rising) flour
75 g (2½ oz) desiccated
  coconut
250 g (8 oz) brown sugar

Topping
25 g (¾ oz) butter
2 tablespoons instant coffee
1¾ cups condensed milk
  (see glossary)
2 tablespoons golden syrup
50 g (1½ oz) chopped
  walnuts

makes 24 squares

Preheat oven to 180°C (350°F). Grease the inside of a slice cake tin (4.5 cm x 3 cm/11 x 7 in).

Melt butter in a saucepan over a low heat. Place flour, coconut and brown sugar into a bowl. Pour melted butter over dry ingredients and mix together. Put the mixture into the tin and press it down all over with the back of a spoon. Bake on the centre shelf of the oven for 20 minutes.

To make the topping, put butter and coffee in a saucepan and melt over a low heat. Add condensed milk and golden syrup and stir over a low heat until thoroughly combined. Add the chopped walnuts and stir through when mixture has cooled. Pour the coffee topping over the cooked base.

* CREPES *

315 ml (1¼ cups) pancake
   batter (see page 326)
butter, for cooking

serves 4–6

Heat a frying pan on low, and add enough butter to cover the bottom liberally. As the pan heats, tilt it to allow butter to run all over the surface. Drain off extra butter, leaving just a film in the pan.

Off the heat, pour in enough batter to run all over pan bottom—about 1 tablespoon for a pan 15 cm (6 in) across. Replace pan over heat and cook until the upper surface of the crepe appears bubbly. Run a small spatula around the edge to loosen the crepe, then slide the knife under and turn or toss crepe over. The side cooked first is served as the outer side.

Turn finished crepes on to a wire rack and cover with a clean tea towel. Stack slightly overlapping and wrap to keep warm.

Serve with jam and freshly whipped cream or lemon juice and sugar.

* CUSTARD *

60 g (2 oz) caster (superfine)
  sugar
1 tablespoon cornflour
  (cornstarch)
2 egg yolks
500 ml (2 cups) milk
piece of lemon rind, finely
  peeled
vanilla essence (optional)

serves 4–6

Mix sugar, cornflour and egg yolks in a small
saucepan with enough of the milk to make a paste,
then add remaining milk and lemon rind. Bring just
to the boil, stirring continuously until thickened.

Remove from heat. Add a little vanilla essence,
to taste (if using). Pour custard into serving jug or
bowl. Cover the top of the jug or bowl with a piece of
greaseproof paper or plastic clingwrap and chill until
serving time.

* DATE SLICE *

125 g (4 oz) self-raising
  (self-rising) flour
60 g (2 oz) desiccated
  coconut
60 g (2 oz) caster (superfine)
  sugar
150 g (5 oz) dates, chopped
125 g (4 oz) butter
lemon frosting (see page 348)

makes 24 squares

Preheat oven to 180°C (350°F). Sift flour into a bowl
and mix in coconut, sugar and dates. Melt butter in
a saucepan over a low heat. Add melted butter to dry
mixture and mix thoroughly with a wooden spoon.
Put mixture into a greased slice tin and press down
firmly with the back of a spoon. Place slice on the
centre shelf of the oven and bake for 25 minutes.

Remove slice from oven and cover with lemon
frosting while it is still hot. Cut into squares while it
is still warm, but leave it in the tin to cool.

* FAIRY CAKES *

125 g (4 oz) butter
150 g (5 oz) caster
 (superfine) sugar
2 eggs
250 g (8 oz) self-raising
 flour, sifted
125 ml (½ cup) milk

makes 25 cakes

Preheat oven to 190°C (375°F). Place butter and sugar into a large bowl and beat together with a wooden spoon until creamy. Beat eggs (one at a time) into butter and sugar. Slowly stir in flour and milk. Stir to remove any lumps.

If using a muffin tin, grease each hollow and sprinkle lightly with flour. If using paper patty cases, place them side by side on a flat tray. Place a heaped teaspoonful of the cake mixture into each patty case. Place the tray in the centre of the oven and bake for 15 minutes.

When the cakes are cool, you can ice them and cover them with sprinkles or make them into butterfly cakes (see page 246).

* FRUIT CRUMBLE *

500 g (1 lb) stewed or
  canned fruit

Topping
125 g (4 oz) plain (all-
  purpose) flour
50 g (1⅔ oz) hard butter
75 g (2½ oz) caster
  (superfine) sugar

serves 6

Preheat oven to 180°C (350°F). If using canned fruit, drain off all the juice. Place fruit in a 20 cm (8 in) ovenproof dish.

Sift flour into a bowl. Grate the butter over the flour and mix through with a knife. Sprinkle sugar over flour and butter and mix again with a wooden spoon. Sprinkle crumble mixture over fruit and press down lightly with a spoon. Put the fruit crumble on the centre shelf of the oven. Bake for 35 minutes, or until the top is golden brown.

✳ GRANDMA'S CHRISTMAS CAKE ✳

250 g (8 oz) dates
250 g (8 oz) raisins
220 g (7 oz) currants
220 g (7 oz) dried pineapple
220 g (7 oz) dried figs
750 ml (3 cups) water
180 g (6 oz) wholemeal flour
375 (12 oz) self-raising (self-
   raising) flour, sifted
180 ml (¾ cup) olive oil

serves 16–20

Chop all fruit and soak in water for 1 hour. Drain off water, reserving 125 ml (½ cup) of the liquid.

Preheat oven to 130°C (265°F). In a bowl, mix flour, reserved water and oil to a soft dough. Add soaked fruit and mix thoroughly. Spread mixture into a greased 25 cm (10 in) square cake tin and cover with foil. Bake in the oven for 3½ hours, removing the foil after 3 hours of cooking. The cake is ready when a wooden skewer inserted into the middle of the cake comes out clean.

* GRAND MARNIER APRICOT BALLS *

250 g (8 oz) dried apricots, finely chopped
45 g (1½ oz) desiccated coconut
150 ml (⅔ cup) condensed milk
½ cup walnuts, chopped
1½ tablespoons preserved ginger, chopped
1 teaspoon lemon rind, grated
1 tablespoon Grand Marnier
extra coconut

makes about 30

In a bowl, combine all ingredients except extra coconut and mix well. Roll teaspoonfuls of the mixture into small balls. Roll balls in extra coconut. Arrange balls on a plastic-covered tray and refrigerate for at least 2 hours or until the balls are firm.

Store in an airtight container in the refrigerator.

Note: These will keep well for about 2 weeks.

* LATTICE TART *

150 g (5 oz) self-raising
   (self-rising) flour
100 g (3½ oz) hard butter
1 egg yolk
2–3 tablespoons milk
5–6 tablespoons strawberry
   jam

serves 4

Preheat oven to 200°C (400°F). Sift flour into a bowl and grate butter over top. Mix gently with a round-bladed knife until blended. Stir in egg yolk and milk, and with floured fingers form mixture into a ball. Place pastry ball onto a floured board and knead lightly. Roll out pastry to 6 mm (¼ in) thickness, so that it will fit over a 20 cm (8 in) pie dish. You need a piece about 5 cm larger in diameter than the pie dish, to allow for the depth of the dish.

Carefully fold pastry over a rolling pin and lower it into pie dish. Press it down around the base and then around the top edge. Trim edge with a knife. Try to keep the edge even. Put pastry scraps back into bowl and form into a ball.

Spoon jam into pastry shell and spread it evenly with a knife. Do not fill pastry shell to the top—the jam will boil over.

Roll out remaining pastry on the floured board into a rectangle. Cut pastry into strips 1 cm (½ in) wide and lay them in a criss-cross pattern over the jam.

Place the lattice tart on the centre shelf of the oven and bake for 20 minutes, or until pastry is golden brown. Serve cool.

* LEMON MERINGUE PIE *

185 g (6 oz) short crust
  pastry (see page 345)

Filling
3 dessertspoons cornflour
  (cornstarch) or custard
  powder
315 ml (1¼ cups) water
60 g (2 oz) margarine
90–120 g (3–4 oz) caster
  (superfine) sugar
2 egg yolks
2 lemons

Meringue
2 egg whites
60 g (2 oz) caster (superfine)
  sugar

serves 4

Preheat oven to 220°C (420°F). Line a pie dish with
the pastry and bake blind for 20–25 minutes. Reduce
oven temperature to 120°C (250°F).

To make the filling, blend cornflour with cold
water in a saucepan. Cook gently until thickened.
Add margarine, sugar and egg yolks. Finely grate zest
of lemons, then juice lemons. Stir zest and juice into
mixture. Pour into the pastry case.

In a bowl, whisk egg whites until they are stiff, then
fold in nearly all the sugar. Pile on top of the lemon
filling and dust with the remaining sugar. Bake for
45 minutes in the oven at the lower temperature, until
the meringue feels firm to the touch. If you bake the
meringue more quickly, it will not stay crisp when cold.

* PANCAKES WITH MAPLE SYRUP *

125 g (4 oz) self-raising
  (self-rising) flour
pinch of salt
½ teaspoon bicarbonate of
  soda (baking soda)
250 ml (1 cup) milk
3 tablespoons caster
  (superfine) sugar
1 egg
butter, for pan
bottle of maple syrup

makes 8

Place flour, salt, bicarbonate of soda, milk, sugar and egg in a jug and beat together until there are no lumps.

Melt a small piece of butter in a frying pan over a medium heat. Pour a little pancake mixture into the centre of the pan—the mixture should spread out to about 15 cm (6 in) across. Cook until the bubbles on top have burst, then flip the pancake over using a spatula. Cook for another minute or two, till underside is golden brown, then lift the pancake onto a plate. Repeat until all mixture is used.

As pancakes are cooked, stack them on a plate, cover with aluminium foil and put in a very slow oven (100°C/200°F) to keep warm. Serve with maple syrup.

Variation: Serve with lemon and sugar or fresh berries instead of maple syrup.

* PATTY CAKES *

90 g (3 oz) butter
90 g (3 oz) caster (superfine)
  sugar
½ teaspoon vanilla essence
2 eggs
180 g (6 oz) self-raising
  (self-rising) flour
pinch of salt
2 tablespoons milk

**makes 20 medium-sized
patties**

Preheat oven to 220°C (420°F). In a bowl, beat together butter, sugar and vanilla essence until mixture is light and fluffy. Add eggs one at a time, beating well after each addition.

In another bowl, sift flour and salt together. Add to butter and sugar mixture, a little at a time, alternately with milk. Mix well after each addition.

Spoon mixture into greased patty tins or patty cases. Bake in the oven for 12–15 minutes.

Allow cakes to cool, then decorate them with warm icing, or make them into butterfly cakes or baskets.

For butterfly cakes, cut a slice (1–1.5 cm/½ in) off the top of each cake, then place a spoonful of cream on the cake, then cut the top in half and place the pieces on the cream at an angle, to represent the wings of butterflies.

* PEANUT BRITTLE CRUMBLE *

6 cooking apples, peeled and
  sliced
2 tablespoons lemon juice
½ teaspoon lemon rind,
  grated
60 g (2 oz) butter
60 g (2 oz) flour
125 g (4 oz) brown sugar
¼ cup smooth peanut butter

serves 6–8

Preheat oven to 180°C (350°F). Place apples in a
20 cm (8 in) pie dish and sprinkle with lemon juice
and rind.

  In a bowl, rub butter into flour with your
fingertips, until mixture is crumbly. Add sugar and
mix well. Using two knives, add peanut butter.

  Sprinkle crumb mixture over apples and bake
in the oven for 30–40 minutes, or until apples are
tender.

  Serve warm, topped with vanilla custard sauce (see
page 376), whipped cream or ice cream.

* PIKELETS *

1 egg
125 g (4 oz) self-raising
  (self-rising) flour, sifted
pinch of salt
¼ teaspoon bicarbonate of
  soda (baking soda) (see
  glossary)
165 ml (⅔ cup) milk
1 teaspoon vinegar
3 tablespoons caster
  (superfine) sugar
2 tablespoons butter

serves 6

In a bowl, beat egg, then add flour, salt, bicarbonate of soda, milk, vinegar and sugar. Mix until smooth.

Melt butter in a frying pan and pour mixture in a tablespoon at a time to cook. When you see bubbles forming at the side of the pikelet, flip the pikelet and cook it for another minute. Continue until you have used all the mixture.

* RAISIN OATMEAL MUFFINS *

125 g (4 oz) plain (all-
  purpose) flour
3 teaspoons baking powder
  (see glossary)
¼ teaspoon salt
60 g (2 oz) butter
100 g (3½ oz) rolled oats
125 g (4 oz) brown sugar,
  firmly packed
125 g (4 oz) raisins
250 ml (1 cup) milk
1 egg, beaten
2 tablespoons caster
  (superfine) sugar
½ teaspoon cinnamon

makes 24

Preheat oven to 200°C (400°F). Sift flour, baking powder and salt together into a bowl, then rub in butter with your fingertips, until mixture resembles fine breadcrumbs. Add rolled oats, brown sugar, raisins, milk and egg, and mix well.

In a cup, combine sugar and cinnamon.

Pour mixture into deep, greased patty pans so that they are all three-quarters full, and sprinkle lightly with cinnamon sugar.

Bake in the oven for 18–20 minutes, or until a skewer inserted into the middle of the muffin comes out clean.

* SHORTBREAD BISCUITS *

125 g (4 oz) butter
60 g (2 oz) caster (superfine)
  sugar
1 teaspoon vanilla essence
100 g (3½ oz) plain (all-
  purpose) flour
60 g (2 oz) rice flour
25 g (¾ oz) cornflour
  (cornstarch)

makes 16

Preheat oven to 200°C (400°F). In a bowl, cream butter and sugar, then add vanilla. While mixing, slowly add flours and form a dough.

Place mixture onto a baking tray covered with baking paper. Place tray in the freezer for 10 minutes (or the refrigerator for 20 minutes). Remove mixture from the freezer and cut into desired biscuit shape.

Cook in the oven for about 10 minutes, or until golden.

* STRAWBERRY SHORTCAKE*

125 g (4 oz) butter
125 g (4 oz) caster
  (superfine) sugar
1 egg
1 teaspoon vanilla essence
180 g (6 oz) plain (all-
  purpose) flour
30 g (1 oz) cornflour
  (cornstarch)
2 teaspoons baking powder
  (see glossary)
2 tablespoons milk
2 punnets strawberries,
  crushed leaving some
  whole, to garnish
250 ml (1 cup) fresh cream,
  whipped

serves 6–8

Preheat oven to 180°C (350°F). In a bowl, cream butter and sugar together until light and fluffy. Add egg and vanilla and beat well.

In another bowl, sift dry ingredients. Add to butter and sugar mixture a little at a time, alternately with milk.

Pour mixture to a greased 20 cm (8 in) spring-form cake tin and bake in the oven for 30–35 minutes, until a skewer inserted into the middle of the cake comes out clean.

Remove cake from tin and allow to stand until quite cold, then cut it horizontally, through the centre. Cover the lower half with whipped cream and crushed strawberries in separate layers. Place the other half on top and cover it with whipped cream and the choicest berries, either whole or halved, placing the cut side down on cream.

*VANILLA CREAMED RICE PUDDING *

1 tablespoon short grain rice
625 ml (2½ cups) milk
1 dessertspoon caster
  (superfine) sugar
1 teaspoon butter
5 cm (2 in) vanilla pod,
  seeds removed
2 teaspoons ground nutmeg

serves 6–8

Preheat oven to 155°C (310°F). Stir rice, milk and sugar together in a buttered ovenproof dish. Add vanilla seeds. Sprinkle top with nutmeg. Place on middle shelf of the oven and cook for 2–2½ hours. Stir the pudding gently once or twice during cooking, slipping a spoon under the skin to do so.

Serve hot or cold. When serving cold, remove the skin and sprinkle top with sugar and more nutmeg.

Basics

* FRENCH ONION DIP *

1 packet French onion soup
300 g (1¼ cups) sour cream
1 teaspoon tabasco sauce
  (optional)

Mix all ingredients and serve.

serves 4

* LAYERED SEAFOOD CREAM CHEESE DIP*

250 g (8 oz) cream cheese
125 g (½ cup) sour cream
60 ml (¼ cup) mayonnaise
  (see page 364)
180 g (6 oz) cooked prawns
125–180 ml (½–¾ cup)
  seafood cocktail sauce
250 g (8 oz) mozzarella
  cheese, shredded
1 green capsicum (bell
  pepper), seeds and pith
  removed and diced
4 shallots (scallions), finely
  sliced
1 tomato, seeded and diced

In a bowl, combine cream cheese, sour cream and mayonnaise. Spread mixture in a circle over the base of a serving platter. Layer the remaining ingredients in order over the top. Chill for 1 hour before serving.
    Serve with corn chips or savoury biscuits.

serves 8–10

* BASIC SCONE DOUGH *

250 g (8 oz) plain (all-
    purpose) flour
2½ tablespoons baking
    powder (see glossary)
½ teaspoon salt
60 g (2 oz) butter
185 ml (¾ cup) milk

makes 12 scones

Sift flour, baking powder and salt into a bowl. Cut butter into flour in small pieces and rub in lightly with your fingertips, until mixture resembles very fine breadcrumbs. Make a well in the centre of the flour, pour in milk and mix to a soft dough. Turn dough onto a lightly floured board and knead very lightly until smooth. Roll out to 1 cm (½ in) thickness and use as required. Dough will keep in the refrigerator for 3–4 days.

To cook, place scones close together on a baking tray and cook in the oven at 200°C (450°F) for 10–15 minutes.

* BATTER *

60 g (2 oz) self-raising (self-
    rising) flour
15 g (½ oz) butter, melted
125 ml (½ cup) lukewarm
    water
1 egg white
¼ teaspoon salt

serves 2

Sift flour into a bowl. Make a well in the centre and add butter and water. Beat together until a smooth batter is formed. Let stand until ready to use. Batter will keep in the refrigerator for 5–7 days.

In another bowl, whisk egg white and salt together until stiff. Gently fold into batter and use immediately.

* PASTA DOUGH *

1 tablespoon salt
3 tablespoons olive oil
5 eggs
375 g (12 oz) plain (all-
    purpose) flour

serves 4

Combine salt, olive oil, and eggs in food processor.

Gradually add flour, pulsing to mix. Use a pasta machine to thin out and cut the dough. Start with a small piece of dough and knead it down until fairly flat. Feed it through the machine at the #1 setting. It's thin enough to use when you can see your hand behind it. Cut the dough into desired pieces. Let dry on paper toweling. When dry run the dough through the machine to cut it.

* SHORT CRUST PASTRY *

250 g (8 oz) plain (all-
    purpose) flour
½ teaspoon salt
60 g (2 oz) butter
3–4 tablespoons cold water

makes 300 g (10 oz)

Sift flour and salt into a bowl. Cut butter into flour in small pieces and rub into flour lightly with your fingertips, until mixture resembles fine breadcrumbs. Add cold water gradually and mix to a stiff dough— the dough should leave the sides of the bowl cleanly. Knead pastry lightly until smooth. Wrap pastry in plastic clingwrap and chill for 30 minutes. Roll out and use as required.

This pastry will keep well in the refrigerator for 3–4 days.

* YORKSHIRE PUDDING*

250 g (8 oz) plain (all-
  purpose) flour
pinch of salt
1 egg
315 ml (⅔ cup) milk

serves 4–6

Preheat oven to 250°C (485°F). Sift flour and salt together into a bowl. Make a well in the centre and drop egg in. Add half the milk, a little at a time, and gradually stir in the flour from the sides of the bowl, using a wooden spoon. Mix until smooth, then beat batter with the back of the spoon for 5–10 minutes. When thoroughly beaten, air bubbles appear on the surface. Cover batter and allow to stand for 30 minutes.

Stir in remaining milk, to give a thin batter, just before cooking. Grease muffin pans or a shallow square 17.5 cm (9 in) cake tin and place in the oven until oil is smoking hot. Remove muffin pans and quickly pour in batter so that it comes halfway up each pan. Return to the oven and cook until yorkshire pudding is crisp, puffed up and golden brown. Serve at once.

* CHOCOLATE FROSTING*

250 g (8 oz) icing
    (confectioners') sugar
3 tablespoons cocoa
2 teaspoons butter
3 tablespoons hot water

makes 260 g (8 oz)

Sift icing sugar and cocoa into a bowl. Put butter into a second bowl and pour over hot water. Stir to melt the butter. Pour butter and water over icing sugar and cocoa and stir until mixture is smooth. Add a little more cocoa to thicken the icing or warm water to thin it.

Variation:
Mocha Icing: Dissolve 1 teaspoon instant coffee in the butter and hot water and make the icing as above.

* ORANGE OR LEMON FROSTING*

250 g (8 oz) icing
    (confectioners') sugar
4 tablespoons orange juice
    or lemon juice

makes 260 g (8 oz)

Sift icing sugar into a bowl and pour over juice. Stir until the icing is smooth.

* PLAIN FROSTING *

250 g (8 oz) icing
  (confectioners') sugar
2 teaspoons butter
2 tablespoons milk

makes 260 g (8 oz)

Sift icing sugar into a bowl. Add butter and milk and mix until smooth. Colour as desired.

* WARM FROSTING AND VARIATIONS *

125 g (4 oz) icing
  (confectioners') sugar, sifted
1 teaspoon butter
60 ml (¼ cup) warm milk

makes 185 g (6 oz)

Place icing sugar in a bowl and mix to a thick paste with melted butter and a little milk. Heat over boiling water until icing is liquid enough to be poured.

Variations:
Coffee frosting: Add 1 teaspoon coffee essence.
Chocolate frosting: Add 1 tablespoon cocoa.
Mocha frosting: Add ½teaspoon coffee essence and 1 dessertspoon cocoa.
Lemon frosting: Use lemon juice instead of milk.
Orange frosting: Use orange juice instead of milk.

* APPLE SAUCE *

4 large cooking apples, peeled
   and sliced
2 tablespoons caster
   (superfine) sugar
3 cloves
30 g (1 oz) butter

serves 8

Preheat oven to 180°C (350°F). Place apples into an
ovenproof dish, sprinkle with sugar and cloves. Cover
and place in the oven for about 30 minutes, or until
apples are soft. Remove cloves, stir apples until pulpy,
then add butter in small pieces and leave to cool.
   Serve warm or cold with roast pork or duck.

* BARBECUE SAUCE *

30 g (1 oz) butter
1¼ cups onion, finely
   chopped
2 tablespoons brown sugar
1 tablespoon vinegar
1 tablespoon Worcestershire
   sauce
125 ml (½ cup) tomato
   sauce
60 ml (¼ cup) water
2 tablespoons lemon juice

serves 4–6

Melt butter in a saucepan and add onion. Sauté until
golden. Add remaining ingredients and bring to the
boil, then reduce heat and simmer for 15 minutes.
   Serve with barbecued sausages, steak and
hamburgers.

* BÉCHAMEL SAUCE *

315 ml (1¼ cups) milk
1 onion, quartered
1 stalk celery, chopped
1 carrot, chopped
6 black peppercorns
1 blade of mace (see glossary)
1 bay leaf
2 cloves
30 g (1 oz) butter
2 tablespoons plain (all-
  purpose) flour
salt and freshly ground black
  pepper, to taste

serves 6

Place milk, onion, celery, carrot, peppercorns, mace, bay leaf and cloves in the top of a double boiler over gently boiling water. Cover the pan and heat very slowly for 30 minutes. Strain and set milk aside.

Melt butter in a heavy saucepan, stir in flour and cook for 1 minute over a medium heat. Add milk and heat, stirring constantly until boiling. Reduce heat to low and cook for 2 minutes. Season with salt and pepper.

* BÉARNAISE SAUCE *

1 shallot (scallion), chopped
½–1 tablespoons tarragon,
   chopped
sprig thyme
1 bay leaf
2 tablespoons tarragon
   vinegar (see glossary)
2 egg yolks
pinch of cayenne pepper
salt and freshly ground black
   pepper, to taste
1–2 tablespoons lemon juice
   or white wine vinegar
90 g (3 oz) butter

serves 4

In a small saucepan, infuse shallot, a little tarragon, thyme and bay leaf in vinegar for 2 minutes. Bring this mixture to the boil, then simmer for 2–3 minutes. Strain.

Using a double boiler (or a bowl over a saucepan), place the egg yolks, seasonings and lemon juice into the top of the pan. Whisk over hot water until the sauce begins to thicken. Add the butter, in very small pieces, whisking in each piece until completely melted before adding the next—do not allow to boil, or it will curdle. If the sauce is too thick, add a little cream.

✳ BOLOGNAISE SAUCE ✳

*250 g (8 oz) lean steak,
  finely chopped*
*250 g (8 oz) lean pork, finely
  chopped*
*60 g (2 oz) bacon or
  prosciutto, chopped*
1 tablespoon olive oil
*4 cloves garlic, peeled and
  chopped*
1 large onion, finely chopped
1 tablespoon parsley, chopped
*1 x 500 g (16 oz) can whole
  tomatoes, peeled*
*250 ml (1 cup) red wine
  (optional)*
125 ml (½ cup) water
2 tablespoons tomato paste
*salt and freshly ground black
  pepper, to taste*
1 bay leaf
½ bunch fresh basil, chopped

serves 4

In a bowl, mix steak, pork and bacon together well. Heat oil in a saucepan, then add meat, garlic, onion and parsley and fry until meat is cooked.

Add tomatoes (with juice from can), wine, water, tomato paste, salt and pepper and bay leaf. Cover and simmer for 1–2 hours. Remove bay leaf and add basil 5 minutes before the end of cooking time.

The longer the sauce is cooked, the more flavour it will have. Check that the sauce isn't drying up while cooking. If necessary, add more wine or water.

* CAVIAR MAYONNAISE *

250 ml (1 cup) mayonnaise
  (see page 364)
250 g (1 cup) sour cream
1 tablespoon lemon juice
2 teaspoons French mustard
30 g (1 oz) black caviar
salt and freshly ground black
  pepper, to taste

serves 6

Combine all ingredients in a bowl and mix together well.

* CHOCOLATE SAUCE *

60 g (2 oz) chocolate,
  roughly chopped
150 ml (⅔ cup) boiling
  water
1 tablespoon cornflour
  (cornstarch)
2 tablespoons cold water
250 g (8 oz) caster
  (superfine) sugar
60 g (2 oz) butter
60 ml (¼ cup) brandy or
  rum (optional)

serves 6–8

Add chocolate to simmering water in a saucepan. Heat gently until chocolate melts and mixture is smooth. In a cup, blend cornflour to a smooth paste with cold water. Add sugar, then cornflour paste, to chocolate mixture. Bring to the boil, stirring continuously until sugar is dissolved and sauce has thickened. Simmer for 3 minutes, then stir in butter and brandy or rum (if using).

* DILL SAUCE *

60 g (2 oz) softened butter
1 teaspoon lemon juice
½ teaspoon dried dill
250 ml (1 cup) mayonnaise
  (see page 364)
½ teaspoon caster (superfine)
  sugar

serves 10

In a bowl, blend softened butter with remaining ingredients, and beat well. Transfer mixture to a saucepan and heat gently. Do not boil. Serve with chicken or lamb.

* FRENCH DRESSING *

3 parts oil
1 part vinegar
salt and freshly ground black
  pepper, to taste

serves 6

Crushed garlic, French or English mustard and chopped herbs can be added. Garlic, mustard, salt and pepper are first mixed with the oil, then vinegar is added and all are well mixed. Herbs are added last.

* GRAPEFRUIT BUTTER *

500 g (1 lb) caster
 (superfine) sugar
125 g (4 oz) butter
250 ml (1 cup) grapefruit
 juice
2 teaspoons grapefruit rind,
 finely grated
5 eggs, well beaten

makes about 1 L (4 cups)

Place sugar, butter, grapefruit juice and rind into the top of a double boiler. Stir over simmering water until butter is melted and sugar is dissolved.

Add eggs and keep stirring over simmering water until mixture thickens and coats the back of a spoon (about 1 hour).

Bottle mixture in sterilised jars. Seal and label. Grapefruit butter will keep well in the refrigerator for 2 weeks.

* GRAVY *

pan juices from roast meat
2–3 tablespoons plain (all-
 purpose) flour
500 ml (2 cups) beef stock
 (see page 378), or water
salt and pepper, to taste

serves 6–8

After removing the roast (see page 188) from your baking tray, leave in about 250 ml (1 cup) of pan juices to make the gravy.

Place the tray on the stove-top, over a medium heat, and sprinkle flour over pan juices. Stir with a wooden spoon until mixture thickens. Add stock, stirring constantly, and simmer gently for 5–10 minutes. Add a little extra stock or water if necessary. Season with salt or pepper.

* HOLLANDAISE SAUCE *

2 egg yolks
pinch of cayenne pepper
salt and freshly ground black
 pepper, to taste
1–2 tablespoons lemon juice
 or white wine vinegar
90 g (3 oz) butter

serves 4–6

Put egg yolks, seasonings and lemon juice into the top of a double boiler, and water into the bottom. Bring water to the boil. Whisk mixture over boiling water until sauce begins to thicken. Add butter, in very small pieces, whisking in each piece until completely melted before adding the next—do not allow sauce to boil, or it will curdle. If the sauce is too thick, add a little cream.

* HONEYED LEMON BUTTER *

5 eggs, well beaten
125 ml (½ cup) honey
125 g (4 oz) butter, softened
250 g (8 oz) caster
 (superfine) sugar
250 ml (1 cup) lemon juice
2 teaspoons lemon rind,
 finely grated

**makes about 750 ml
(3 cups)**

Combine all ingredients in top of double boiler. Stir over simmering water until thickened (about 1 hour).
 Bottle mixture in sterilised jars. Seal and label. Honeyed Lemon Butter will keep well in the refrigerator for 2 weeks.

* HORSERADISH CREAM *

250 ml (1 cup) fresh cream
salt and ground black pepper,
   to taste
pinch of paprika
125 ml (½ cup) horseradish
   relish
1 tablespoon chives, chopped

serves 4–6

In a bowl, whip cream until stiff, then fold in remaining ingredients. Chill for half an hour before serving. Serve with roast meat, steak or potatoes.

* CUCUMBER SOUR CREAM SAUCE*

1 green cucumber, peeled and
   seeds removed
1 x 300 g (9 oz) carton sour
   cream
1 clove garlic, crushed
1 tablespoon lemon juice
pinch of ground black pepper

makes 375 ml (1¼ cups)

Chop cucumber roughly and place in blender or food processor with half the sour cream. Cover and blend for a few seconds. Place blended mixture in a bowl and stir in remaining sour cream, garlic, lemon juice and pepper. Serve with new potatoes or as a dressing for potato salad.

Note: For a thinner consistency, blend all the sour cream with the cucumber in the beginning.

* ITALIAN TOMATO SAUCE *

2 tablespoons olive oil
1 small onion, finely chopped
2 cloves garlic, crushed
1 kg (2 lb) tomatoes,
  skinned, seeded and
  chopped or 2 x 440 g
  (14 oz) can whole
  tomatoes, diced
½ teaspoon salt
½ teaspoon caster (superfine)
  sugar, or to taste
¼ teaspoon freshly ground
  black pepper
2 leaves basil
1 sprig oregano
1 bay leaf
1 tablespoon tomato paste

serves 4

In a large saucepan, heat oil. Add onion and garlic and cook for 5–6 minutes, stirring until onion is translucent. Add tomatoes and all other ingredients. Return to heat and bring to the boil. Reduce heat, cover, and simmer for 45 minutes, stirring occasionally.

Purée sauce in a blender or food processor if you want a smooth consistency.

* MAYONNAISE *

1–2 egg yolks
1 teaspoon white wine
   vinegar
½ teaspoon salt
½ teaspoon dry mustard (see
   glossary)
pinch of white pepper
150 ml (⅔ cup) olive oil
few drops of lemon juice

make 250 ml (1 cup)

Make sure your bowl is well washed and dried. In it beat egg yolks, vinegar, salt, dry mustard and pepper with an egg beater or an electric beater set at medium speed.

Add olive oil, drop by drop, whisking continuously, until about 2 tablespoons have been added. Add a few drops of lemon juice, to bring mixture to the consistency of cream. Add the remaining oil in a thin steady stream, beating continuously, stopping the addition of the oil from time to time to make sure the mixture is combining well.

When all the oil has been added and the mayonnaise is thick, add extra lemon juice to taste. Adjust seasoning. Mayonnaise will keep for 5–7 days in a sealed container in the refrigerator.

Note: If the mixture curdles, wash the beater, beat 1 egg yolk in another bowl and very slowly add the curdled mayonnaise to the fresh egg yolk, beating continuously.

* MINT SAUCE *

2 heaped tablespoons
  mint leaves
2 teaspoons caster (superfine)
  sugar
½ teaspoon hot water
2 tablespoons vinegar

serves 2

Wash and dry mint leaves, then put them on a chopping board with 1 teaspoon sugar (this helps you chop the mint finely). Chop until fine, then put into a sauceboat. Add the rest of the sugar, stir in the hot water and leave for a few minutes, to dissolve sugar. Add the vinegar.

* PARSLEY BUTTER *

60 g (2 oz) butter
1 teaspoon parsley, finely
  chopped
2 teaspoons lemon juice

makes 65 g (2 oz)

In a bowl, beat the butter until light and creamy. Beat in parsley and lemon juice. Chill well before serving.

* PEANUT SAUCE *

60 g (2 oz) butter
1 onion, finely chopped
1 clove garlic, crushed
1 tablespoon soy sauce
1 tablespoon peanut butter
1 teaspoon lemon juice
125 ml (½ cup) fresh cream

makes 300 ml (1¼ cups)

Heat butter in a saucepan, then sauté onion and garlic until golden. Add soy sauce, peanut butter and lemon juice and mix thoroughly. Remove sauce from heat and cool. Before serving, add the cream. This sauce is delicious with barbecued steak and chops.

* PLUM SAUCE *

250 g (8 oz) plum jam
75 ml (¼ cup) mango
  chutney
75 ml (¼ cup) mango nectar
1 tablespoon vinegar
1 teaspoon caster (superfine)
  sugar

makes 400 ml (1½ cups)

In a bowl, mix plum jam with mango chutney and nectar. Purée mixture in a blender or food processor. In a saucepan, heat vinegar, add sugar and stir until dissolved. Add jam mixture and beat well.

* QUICK TOMATO SAUCE *

30 g (1 oz) butter
1 small onion, grated
1 small apple, grated
2 teaspoons cornflour
  (cornstarch)
315 ml (1¼ cups) water
salt and freshly ground black
  pepper, to taste
1 x 150 g (5 oz) can tomato paste
good pinch of caster
  (superfine) sugar

Heat butter in a saucepan. Fry onion for a few minutes, then the apple until soft. In a bowl, blend cornflour with water and salt and pepper. Add tomato paste and cornflour mixture to saucepan. Bring mixture to the boil and stir until smooth and thickened. Simmer gently for about 10 minutes, then taste, adjust seasonings and add sugar. Serve warm.

makes 500 ml (2 cups)

* SALAD DRESSING *

1 lemon juice
2 tablespoons Dijon mustard
250 ml (1 cup) olive oil
1 teaspoon salt
80 ml (⅓ cup) balsamic
  vinegar
1 clove garlic, crushed
1 teaspoon fresh basil, finely
  chopped

In a bowl, mix all ingredients well until combined.

makes 375 ml (1½ cups)

* SEAFOOD DRESSING *

125 ml (½ cup) tomato
   ketchup
125 g (½ cup) mayonnaise
   (see page 364)
1 x 125 ml (4 fl oz) fresh
   cream

serves 4

Mix all ingredients together and chill before serving.
   Dressing will keep well in the refrigerator for
5–7 days.

* STRAWBERRY OR RASPBERRY SAUCE*

125 ml (½ cup) strawberry
   or raspberry juice
1 tablespoon redcurrant jelly,
   warmed
1 teaspoon cornflour
   (cornstarch)

serves 4–6

Place juice in a saucepan, reserving 1 tablespoon.
Add redcurrant jelly and bring mixture to the boil.
In a cup or small bowl, blend cornflour with reserved
juice to make a paste. Pour a little hot juice onto
blended mixture, stirring with a wooden spoon. Pour
cornflour mixture into saucepan and boil mixture,
stirring continuously, until sauce is clear and has
thickened. Serve with ice cream or cake.
   This sauce will keep well in the refrigerator for 3–4
days.

* SWEET AND SOUR SAUCE *

1 tablespoon cornflour
  (cornstarch)
1 tablespoon soy sauce
185 ml (¾ cup) white
  vinegar
185 ml (¾ cup) caster
  (superfine) sugar
250 ml (1 cup) chicken stock
  (see page 380)
1 green capsicum (bell
  pepper), seeded and sliced
250 g (1 cup) pineapple
  pieces
1 small carrot, thinly sliced
1 teaspoon fresh ginger, finely
  chopped

serves 6–8

In a cup, blend cornflour and soy sauce together until smooth. Place in a sauce-pan with vinegar, sugar and chicken stock. Bring to the boil, stirring continuously. Simmer for 5 minutes.

Meanwhile, blanch capsicum and drain it. Add pineapple, capsicum, carrot and ginger to sauce. Heat gently and serve immediately.

* TARTARE SAUCE *

150 ml (⅔ cup) mayonnaise
  (see page 364)
1 teaspoon capers, chopped
1 teaspoon gherkin, chopped
1 teaspoon parsley, freshly
  chopped
½ teaspoon dried tarragon
½ teaspoon dried chervil
pinch of caster (superfine)
  sugar
salt and freshly ground black
  pepper, to taste

serves 4

Combine all ingredients and season with salt and
pepper. This sauce is delicious served with oysters,
prawns or fillets of fish. Keeps in the refrigerator for
5–7 days.

☀ THOUSAND ISLAND DRESSING ☀

*250 ml (1 cup) mayonnaise
(see page 364)*
2 tablespoons tomato ketchup
*2 tablespoons chilli sauce
(optional)*
*2 tablespoons green olives,
finely chopped*
*1 tablespoons chives, finely
chopped*
2 tablespoons whipped cream

serves 6

In a bowl, combine all ingredients well. Chill before
serving.

* VANILLA CUSTARD SAUCE *

315 ml (½ pint) milk
½ teaspoon vanilla essence
3 tablespoons caster sugar
3 egg yolks

serves 4–6

In a saucepan, heat milk over a low heat. Add vanilla essence and stir through. In a bowl, mix sugar and egg yolks until smooth. Add a little of the warmed milk to the egg mixture, stirring constantly, then add remaining milk.

Return mixture to the saucepan, still on a low heat, and stir constantly, until the mixture thickens and has the consistency of cream (it should coat the back of a metal spoon). Serve warm with ice cream, baked and steamed puddings or fruit puddings.

This sauce will keep well in the refrigerator for 3–4 days.

* WHITE SAUCE *

30 g (1 oz) butter
30 g (1 oz) plain (all-
   purpose) flour
315 ml (1¼ cups) milk
salt
nutmeg or freshly ground
   black pepper, to taste

serves 4–6

Melt butter in a saucepan over a low heat, then remove from heat and stir in flour. Return to heat and cook gently for a few minutes, making sure that the roux does not brown. Remove pan from heat and gradually blend in cold milk. Replace pan on heat and bring to the boil. Reduce heat and cook, stirring with a wooden spoon, until smooth. Season well. If any lumps have formed, whisk briskly.

Variation: The amount of milk you use determines the consistency of the sauce. For coating consistency use 315 ml (1¼ cups) milk; for a thin sauce for soups use 625 ml (2½ cups); and for binding consistency use 150 ml (⅔ cup).

* BEEF STOCK *

1 kg (2 lb) shin of beef,
  finely sliced
3.8 L (6 pints) cold water
60 g (2 oz) butter
1 carrot, thinly sliced
1 parsnip, thinly sliced
1 turnip, thinly sliced
1 onion, thinly sliced
2 stalks celery, thinly sliced
1 large tomato, finely
  chopped
salt and freshly ground black
  pepper, to taste

makes 3.8 L (6 pints)

Place beef in a large saucepan. Add water, making sure it covers beef, and bring to the boil. Cover and simmer for 30 minutes. Chill. Remove surface fat, skim off floating particles and strain.

Melt butter in a large saucepan and fry vegetables over a moderate heat for 10 minutes, being careful not to let onion burn. Add strained liquid and salt and pepper, then bring liquid to the boil. Simmer, covered, for 2 hours. Strain stock. Let it cool, and keep it in the refrigerator.

Will keep up to 3 days in the refrigerator or 3 months in the freezer.

* CHICKEN STOCK *

1 chicken, fat removed
3.8 L (6 pints) cold water
1 carrot
1 parsnip
4 stalks celery
1 white onion
60 g (2 oz) butter
6 sprigs parsley
salt and freshly ground black
    pepper, to taste

makes 3.8 L (6 pints)

Place chicken in a large saucepan. Add water, making sure it covers chicken, and bring to the boil. Cover and simmer for 30 minutes, then chill. Remove surface fat and strain liquid. Rinse semi-cooked carcass with warm water.

Cut vegetables into 5 mm (¼ in) slices. Melt butter in a large saucepan and fry vegetables over moderate heat for 10 minutes. Do not let onion burn. Add strained liquid together with chicken and parsley. Simmer, covered, for 2 hours, skimming surface occasionally. Add salt and pepper. Remove chicken and strain stock. Cool stock and store in the refrigerator.

* COURT BOUILLON *

375 ml (1½ cups) water
125 ml (½ cup) white wine
juice of 1 lemon
1 onion, chopped
½ celery stick, chopped
1 garlic clove, finely chopped
1 teaspoon black peppercorns
4 to 5 sprigs fresh thyme
1 bay leaf

makes 500 ml (2 cups)

Combine all ingredients in a saucepan and bring to a boil over high heat. Reduce heat and simmer for 8 minutes. Strain or use chunky the first time, then purée in a blender or food processor and either refrigerate for up to 3 days or freeze for up to 2 months. Either way, be sure to bring to a boil before reusing.

* FISH STOCK *

750 g (1½ lb) fish bones and
   trimmings
1 tomato, chopped
2 sprigs parsley
1 bay leaf
1 large onion, sliced
1 clove garlic, crushed
2 teaspoons salt
6 black peppercorns
2.2 L (3½ pints) cold water

makes 2.2 L (3½ pints)

Wash fish bones or trimmings well. Place in a large saucepan with other ingredients. Cover saucepan and bring to the boil. Reduce heat and simmer for 1 hour. Strain before using.

* BREADCRUMB STUFFING *
(FOR FISH)

4 tablespoons soft white
  breadcrumbs
1 teaspoon parsley, finely
  chopped
½ teaspoon lemon rind,
  grated
¼ teaspoon dried mixed
  herbs
1 teaspoon anchovies
15 g (½ oz) melted butter
salt and freshly ground black
  pepper, to taste
a little beaten egg or milk, to
  bind

In a bowl, mix all ingredients.

Loosely stuff cavity of fish and close opening with toothpicks before baking or barbecueing.

Variation: Use a few chopped prawns, oysters or sliced, sautéed mushrooms instead of the mixed herbs.

* CHICKEN STUFFING *

4 tablespoons breadcrumbs
2–3 cloves garlic, chopped
1 tablespoon parsley, chopped
¼ teaspoon mixed herbs
1 onion, finely chopped
¼ teaspoon salt
pinch of pepper
1 egg, beaten
½ cup lemon juice
grated rind of 1 lemon

In a mixing bowl, combine breadcrumbs, garlic, parsley, mixed herbs, onion, salt and pepper and mix well. Add egg, lemon juice and lemon rind and stir until well combined.

GLOSSARY

Allspice: The dried berry of the pimiento tree. The dried berries are dark brown and are available whole or ground. The whole berries are used in pickles, preserves and chutney and when ground as a flavouring in cakes, soups and meat dishes.

Ascorbic acid: Scientific name for vitamin C. Used to prevent the browning of vegetables and fruit.

Baking powder: A leavener containing a mixture of baking soda and cornstarch. When mixed with liquid it releases carbon dioxide gas bubbles that cause a bread or cake to rise.

Bicarbonate of soda: Also known as baking soda, this is used as a leavener in baked foods.

Bouquet garni: A bundle of herbs tied together with string. Commonly used to flavour soups, sauces and stews. The herbs are usually parsley, thyme and a bay leaf.

Cardamom: An aromatic spice with a spicy-sweet flavour. Cardamom is used in Indian curries and Scandinavian cakes and pastries. The seeds can be bought separately but it is better to buy the pods and seed them yourself, as they lose their flavour quickly once removed from the pod.

Celery salt: Seasoning of blended ground celery seed and salt.

Condensed milk: Evaporated milk that has had its water content reduced, and has been sweetened and thickened with sugar.

Copha: A shortening agent made from coconut oil that has been processed into a white waxy solid.

Cream of tartar: An acid compound deposited on the sides of wine barrels during wine-making. When purified and chrystallised it is called cream of tartar. An ingredient in baking powder.

Deglazing: Adding water, stock, wine or cream and scraping the bottom of the cooking pan to incorporate the juices and particles of food that has been cooked into a liquid and simmering until a sauce has formed.

Dill pickles: Pickles preserved in seasoned brine or vinegar and dill.

Dry mustard: Finely ground mustard seeds, also referred to as powdered mustard. Used to flavour meats and vegetables or as an ingredient in salad dressings.

Evaporated milk: Milk that has had its water content reduced by evaporation, making it thicker than ordinary milk.

Fricassee: A meat dish that has been sautéed in butter before being stewed with vegetables.

Garam masala: A blend of ground spices used in Indian cuisine. Might contain coriander seeds, cumin seeds, cardamom seeds, peppercorns, cinnamon sticks, cloves and nutmeg.

Glucose syrup: A mixture of sugars derived from starch. Used as a sweetener in drinks and desserts.

Glycerine: Commercial name for a colourless, syrupy liquid obtained from fats and oils. It is used to retain moisture and add sweetness to food.

Grapeseed oil: An oil extracted from grape seeds, which is commonly used in salad dressings.

Mace: The red membrane that surrounds nutmeg. It is a pungent spice used in chutneys, pickles and sauces.

Marsala: A rich, smoky-flavoured fortified wine from Sicily. Flavour ranges from sweet to dry.

Maryland: The combined thigh and drumstick of a chicken.

Melba toast: Very thin, crisp toast used to accompany soups or salads.

Mirepoix: Diced vegetables (carrots, onions and celery) fried in butter and herbs. Often used to flavour stocks, sauces and stews or as a garnish on meat or poultry.

Mustard seeds: Seeds from the mustard plant used as a seasoning or in pickling. Mustard seeds are sold whole or ground, and are used to make mustard.

Pesto: Sauce made from puréed fresh basil, garlic, pine nuts and olive oil. Commonly used as a spread or a pasta sauce.

Pink peppercorns: Pungent and slightly sweet berries from the Baies rose plant. Available freeze-dried or packed in brine.

Preserved ginger: Ginger which has been preserved in a sugar-salt mixture. Available from Asian food stores and supermarkets.

Ragoût: A French stew made with poultry or meat and vegetables.

Ramekins: Individual porcelain baking dishes usually 7.5–10 cm (3–4 in) in diameter.

Saffron: The stigmas of the crocus flower. Gold in colour, it is an aromatic spice with a pungent, slightly bitter flavour. Used in paella and bouillabaise.

Scalding: To heat a liquid to almost boiling point so that small bubbles form around the edge of the pan and a film appears over the surface of the liquid.

Seasoned flour: Plain flour with a pinch of salt and pepper mixed through. Mixed herbs can also be added for a more intense flavour.

Sherry vinegar: A mellow vinegar made from sherry. Often used as a vinaigrette or to deglaze a roasting pan to make gravy.

Tarragon vinegar: Vinegar steeped with the herb tarragon.

Truss: To secure meat or poultry with string or skewers so that the food maintains its shape during cooking.

Vanilla: Derived from the dried seed-pod of an orchid plant found in Central America. The vanilla flavour extracted from the pod is used to enrich cakes, custards, ice cream and other sweet dishes.

Vermicelli: Very fine strands of spaghetti

Vine leaves: The leaves of the grape vine, usually blanched and then preserved in brine or vinegar before being eaten. Young and tender leaves should be used.

Wheat, cracked: Whole wheat grain broken into coarse, medium or fine fragments. Available from health food stores.

Wheat germ: The embryo of a wheat grain. A source of vitamins, minerals and protein. It has a nutty flavour and is very oily. Available from health food stores.

Wonton wrappers: Chinese dish of steamed bite-sized dumplings made of paper-thin sheets of dough pillows filled with a mixture of meat, vegetables or seafood.

WEIGHTS & MEASUREMENTS

Temperature

100°C = 200°F
120°C = 250°F
140°C = 280°F
150°C = 300°F
165°C = 325°F
180°C = 350°F
190°C = 375°F
200°C = 400°F
220°C = 420°F
250°C = 485°F

Fluid measures

60 ml = ¼ cup
85 ml = ⅓ cup
125 ml = ½ cup
250 ml = 1 cup
500 ml = 2 cups
1 L = 1.6 pints

Solid measures

10 g = ⅓ oz
20 g = ⅔ oz
30 g = 1 oz
40 g = 1½ oz
60 g = 2 oz
80 g = 2½ oz
100 g = 3½ oz
120 g = 4 oz
150 g = 5 oz
160 g = 5½ oz
180 g = 6 oz
200 g = 7 oz
250 g = 8 oz
300 g = 10 oz
350 g = 11½ oz
400 g = 14 oz
500 g = 1 lb
750 g = 1½ lb
1kg = 2 lb

INDEX